There were only two things keeping me in Windsor: my family and friends, and my Kung Fu school. That sounds like three things, but it's really one thing.

In the summer of 2000, I moved my love and myself to Toronto to start our new life. I was beginning the job I'd dreamed of, she was switching to a university she favoured, in a city she loved; a city I was quickly growing to like.

However, all my love's talk of marriage, togetherness, and eternity was a lie. She turned out to be nothing more than a cheating slut; a ruthless whore, who'd been sleeping with her history professor. It's hard to believe, I'd thought she was my soul-mate. I was crushed.

Women aren't to be trusted.

To add to my misery, after only 18 days on the job I was fired by the President and Vice-president of the board of directors. Apparently, it was concluded, after this fair chance, that I was not good at the profession of my choice. There was, however, someone available to take my place. The vice-president's son wasn't able to find work in his chosen profession. He stepped in. How fortunate for them.

Suddenly, I was alone and unemployed, broken-hearted and just plain broke in Canada's biggest metropolis.

It has been said, "Life is what happens to you while you're busy making other plans."

So, why make plans?

Order this book online at www.trafford.com
or email orders@trafford.com

Most Trafford titles are also available at major online book retailers.

Printed in Victoria, BC, Canada.

ISBN: 978-1-4269-1971-8

*Our mission is to efficiently provide the world's finest, most comprehensive book publishing
service, enabling every author to experience success. To find out how to publish your book, your
way, and have it available worldwide, visit us online at www.trafford.com*

Trafford rev. 12/16/2009

 www.trafford.com

North America & international
toll-free: 1 888 232 4444 (USA & Canada)
phone: 250 383 6864 ♦ fax: 812 355 4082

Living Tao,

Living Kung Fu,

Living My Life

Do not be misled by my title.

I do not claim to have fully abided in the Tao. This is virtually impossible for anyone.

Herein, I simply guide the willing reader through a sliver of my life at a time when I sought to remember myself.

During the course of my journal writings I discovered that I was no longer writing to myself, but to a selected audience – an ever-changing audience: my sifu, my friends, my mother, my students, myself, the world in general. Because of this, my writing ceased to be a journal and became merely a collection.

Take from it what you will.

Dedicated to:

Brad Owens, Howard Chang, Simon Pszczonack, and my mom.

Further gratitude goes to:

Kevin Francis, Rich Reid, Simon Merritt, Scotty Landry, Boner, Hilly, Stacey, Tyna, Katie, Janice, Dave, Sean, Jeremy, my family, Laurel Choat, Doolie, Goob, Brian, Frank, Gord, Roger Soo, Mrs. Chang (auntie), Mei-shen, Sabrina, Wu Hung Li (wherever you are), and, of course, the Wu Shen Temple.

Have you seen pictures or footage of those men on oil rigs out on the hot, tropical ocean, working hard while covered in oil? Imagine you're one of them. Now, imagine it's not hot and sunny. It's a cold, wet, Canadian winter. And it's not oil you're covered in... it's human feces. That's construction in a sewage plant.

Ironically, that's the job my buddy, Brad, gave me to keep me from having a nervous breakdown. And I was damn grateful to have it. And damn grateful to have his couch to sleep on at the end of the day.

I've described the job at its worst. Some job sites were quite clean. However; when it was at its most disgusting, that job would bring lesser men to illness. Not these guys. The guys I worked with were a bunch of tough nuts. Despite the conditions, I don't remember more laughter or singing on any other job I've ever had. Even when one of these guys described one of the worst times of his past, he'd have a smile on his face. A lot more people could learn from these blue-collar roughnecks. Some of them are living the Tao, even if they don't know it. To them, I will always be grateful.

"When are you coming back? - a year or two?"

These questions reoccurred regularly in the weeks prior to my departure to Taiwan. I never gave a definitive answer. Years ago, I'd lived in Japan and I returned after one year. I'd made promises that I would not stay longer. Eventually, I regretted it.

I wasn't in love with Japan or its culture, but I was in love with one of its citizens. Mutsumi Shoji is a true lady. I can't imagine any man not falling in love with her. Mu-chan, as I called her, promised to come to Canada two months after me, so we could be together. That promise was broken. Women aren't to be trusted.

I also regretted my promises to return to Canada so soon, because they held me back from other opportunities in Japan. I would not make that mistake again.

Besides, I had resolved myself to living more with the Tao. By that I mean, simply allowing life to happen. Why make plans?

Some thought my going away again was a great idea. Most were not supportive. I was surprised that some of my closest friends protested. Brad, Kevin and Rich seemed to disapprove. Rich's wife, however, admired my sense of adventure. She had always been supportive of me. During my recent heartache, she reassured me that any woman who'd claim to be in love with one man and claiming to want to marry him, while having an affair with another was absolutely insane and not worthy of my love.

It turns out at that time she was cheating on Rich. They had been married only a year and a half. A happy, blissful 18 months, as far as he knew. They are currently separated, awaiting their divorce. Have I mentioned women aren't to be trusted?

I would leave in Mid-February. I would continue to work in the sewage plants until then. In Hamilton, the "waste-water treatment plant" has one of its spherical tanks painted as a giant globe. On one particularly cold, wet day, one of my co-workers caught me staring up at it.

"You're looking to Taiwan, aren't you? You lucky bastard."

Somebody insisted that I would miss Canadian winters. He was wrong. The idea of being somewhere sub-tropical seemed like heaven at this point. I sang of it everyday and imagined it every night.

I arrived in Taipei on February 14th, 2001.

Early April, 2001

As I write this passage, I sit by the pond in front of my residence in Hsin Chuang. It's ideally comfortable. Warm air dances softly, moved by only a hint of a breeze that prevents insects or humidity from disturbing me. It's peaceful, but not quiet. The crickets are loud. They keep a constant mid-pitch drone to underscore the other sounds of pond life. Peepers chirp cheerfully to one another; occasionally overpowered by the base bellow of a bullfrog. It's spring; and they are boasting of virility (as do all males seeking to impress potential partners). The splash of eager fish is an added element to this "non-arrangement."

I resist the writer's temptation to compare it to orchestrated music. It's completely random... patternless notes... perhaps, that's what makes it more beautiful.

I've been busy the past six weeks. Adjusting to my new home, my new job, and my new life-style has been successful. I'm getting comfortable... too comfortable. My training slacked at first, but in the last three weeks I've gradually increased my sessions... only physically, though. I've not meditated in over a month. And only now am I taking the time to reflect on my teaching.

I think of Sifu and I hear his voice:

"Do what you must do, go where you must go, but remember, Kung Fu is always with you, and your school is always here."

Sifu Simon Pszczonack has taught me more about being a warrior, than anyone else on the planet. We are connected. Everywhere I go, I hear him.

It's impossible to describe without conjuring corny images in the reader's mind of a floating Master Po, or of a translucent Obi-Wan Kenobi. When I first became his student, I was in awe of him. Sifu appeared to be a shaolin guru shrouded in ancient mysteries. We were the proverbial eager novice and intangible mentor.

Our relationship is no longer easily defined. We are close friends, yet to explain the proper protocol and etiquette that exists as a result of my role in the kwoon, it would seem complicated. It's not. To us it's simple... strange, but simple.

I hesitate to write these words: I miss him. I hesitate, knowing he may someday read these words, and I will have exposed a weakness.

How strange is that friendship?

That previous passage was interrupted by the arrival of my beautiful, young neighbour, Mei-shen. We have a lot of fun together. We make each other laugh. She became fascinated with me because of interest in Chinese culture. Most of her friends are young, like her (8 years my junior) and they aren't involved in their heritage. But now, she's met a foreigner, whose apartment follows Fung Shuai design, who knows Chinese history and is an instructor of Northern Seven-Star Praying Mantis Shaolin Kung Fu.

I am currently teaching her Kung Fu. We spent the next hour working on a basic form. She does well, but she is frustrated that is still far from perfect. She's impatient with herself; frustrated that she can't make the corrections immediately. She's asking herself to be more than human.

I explain, "this isn't university, its not brain surgery, its not rocket science... this is **really** hard. If it were easy, everyone would know it, and it wouldn't be worthwhile."

Her head knows, but her heart yearns. I feel her frustration because she reminds me of someone I used to know.... someone I'm almost rid of.

She believes she is in love with me. But young women are prone to telling lies - if not to men than to themselves.

She wants to hear me reciprocate those feelings. She'll wait a long time. I've already pushed away a couple of women over the past few months for that kind of behaviour. I haven't done that to Mei-shen... not yet.

I've explained it to her; how I've seen women change from treating me like a deity to treating me like a toilet. How she's given me know reason to think she's different. She's been warned not push me for more than I want to give.

Some readers may wonder how I can be so forthcoming with my distrust. How can I so bluntly tell a romantic interest that I don't trust her? It's a biological condition. There is a factor in my genetic composition that compels me to say things as I perceive them, without twisting vocabulary nor room for misinterpretation... it's called a **Y** chromosome.

Could I love her? I don't know... what's worse yet, I don't care. That's not as harsh as it sounds. I simply mean I'm enjoying things as they are, without expectations. Maybe I'm just in need of companionship and praise. I'm not yet rid of my ego. I don't care. Maybe I'm just holding back because of my past. I don't care. Maybe I'm wrong and fate does exist.... maybe Mei-shen is here to rescue me from distrust with her faithfulness and uncanny wisdom... or maybe fate is a crock of dung invented by philosophers. I don't care. What matters is I'm happy and I'm at peace.

My mother called the other day. She said I sounded like my old self again. By that she meant the happy-go-lucky lad she raised. The one I ceased to be several months ago. I'm thrilled to say she's right. I'm me again. And it feels great.

Our Kung Fu Family

Why Taiwan? Obviously, I've a strong interest in Chinese culture. That would make Mainland China a good choice, except that decades ago Mao Tse Tung's "cultural revolution" put a squeeze on traditional arts and philosophies. Many practitioners fled their motherland. Some returned over this last decade. Most did not. That's why today, it is just as easy to find a qualified Kung Fu instructor in Australia, Argentina, Canada, England, the U.S., etc. as it is in China.

Many practitioners fled to the rebel province, including my teacher's teacher, Wu Heng Li and his teacher Wang Tsung Ching. Wu eventually left Taiwan for Canada. He taught in Ontario for decades. He later retired in B.C. Then, about two years ago, he returned to Taichung, Taiwan.

Another member of our Kung Fu family resides here. My junior brother, Howard is Taiwanese. After 12 years in Canada, he returned to Taipei. This greatly influenced my decision to come here, instead of the mainland.

Howard met me at the airport when I arrived and I stayed with his family for a couple weeks. It was Howard that gave me my Chinese name. His Chinese name is How-Ning, his younger brother is How-Wei (a.k.a. Johnson). It occurred to Howard that since I'm the oldest brother, I should be "How-Jay." Had Howard been sober at the time he created my name, he might have realized he was writing the Chinese word for "natural disaster." I thought it was the perfect name. But Howard convinced me that I should change the characters to mean "outstanding" which is still pronounced the same way. "Outstanding" has some appeal, but it just doesn't have the pizzazz of "natural disaster." - I reluctantly agreed.

I took my surname from the warrior-poet, Sun-Tzu and now, carry the name **Sun How-Jay** on all my official papers.

Howard and I have discussed the idea of trying to locate Sigung Wu Hung Li. No one of our generation has even seen him. The chances of finding a man named Wu, in a city of more than 2 million are slim, but we must at least try.

It's like searching for a grandfather you've never met.

Late April, 2001

Last night, I lay very still and felt like a warrior. I could feel my blood move and hear my heart beat. Within my body, I could feel my internal energies flowing with the power of a great river and the subtlety of the moon passing from one horizon to another.

Continuous forms training have carved muscle into my arms, legs, back and torso. Stance training, breathing exercises and meditation have ignited my chi back into a fire from the embers of which I let it diminish.

In contemplating your cultivation of chi, you may question whether you feel this energy, or whether it is merely psychosomatic. If the results are the same, does it matter?

Yesterday, however, I had more than faith to go on. I went to the gym.

It was the first time in over two months that I had been to weight train, and the six months prior to that, had only been a series of half-hearted attempts to get back into a regimen.

A year ago, this week, I defeated my American counterparts in Cleveland, Ohio to become the North American Shuai-Chiao fighting Champion. That was the last time I felt like a real athlete.

This first time back in a gym should have proven to be a struggle. Instead, I felt sensational. The weights are calibrated in kilograms. Canada is on the metric system, but most gyms still use poundage. I decided not to waste time calculating. I simply threw on more weight with each set until it felt reasonable. I did the math later. "Impossible," I thought. I did the math again. I pressed an amount that I had done before, but that should have been impossible for me at this time. That's one of the capabilities of chi, allowing your body to do what otherwise would be impossible. This was hardly an example of the true significance of chi development. It's only a rudimentary demonstration of a novice cultivator. But I will speak more of the phenomenal results of cultivation further on.

Weight training

What is the value of weight training to a martial artist? Virtually nothing. To an athlete? Much more.

I no longer compete. Now, I train with weights purely for vanity. Being pleased with the way I look when my muscles are bigger is one of my weaknesses. It's that simple.

Cleaning 200lbs. is real explosive power. But holding a horse stance for 10 minutes is real strength. You can build explosive power through martial training alone (even without chi cultivation) but weight training will certainly add to it tremendously.

Weight training is necessary for combat sports; which should not be confused with martial arts.

Combat Sports

Combat sports have rules that eliminate the most dangerous techniques of fighting, **as they should.** To compensate for this hindrance, a fighter needs power. This is why in a real confrontation a 150lb. man has as much a chance as a 200lb. man depending on their level of proficiency. In contrast, combat sports require weight categories to be fair.

To help eliminate the confusion, here is a list of combat sports:

Striking:
Boxing, Kickboxing, Taekwondo, Muay Thai, Sport Karate, Full contact anything.
Which are derived from these martial arts: Karate, Tung Soo Do, Savate, Ancient Muay Thai, Ancient Pankration.

Grappling:
Judo, Wrestling, Sambo, Sumo, Sport Shuai-Chiao.
Which derived from: Ju-jitsu, Hapkido, Ancient Pankration, Traditonal Shuai-Chiao, Chin Na/Kung Fu.

Combination/Submission:
Modern Pancration, X-treme fighting, U.F.C., Pit-fighting, Vale Tudo.
Which derived from: Damn near everything.

(Do I need to mention that Olympic style fencing derived from medieval European fencing? I just know I'm going to get complaints from readers, who love some wonderful but obscure combat sports. I apologize, now, to enthusiasts of jousting, Indian thumb-wrestling, and dodgeball.)

Anyone who believes a combat sport is a martial art is an idiot. But likewise, anyone who believes a person can develop the skills, which make him a world-class combat sport champion without becoming a good fighter, is also an idiot.

Some people are what we call physical geniuses. Because of their incredible reflexes, coordination and awareness they could be great at any physical endeavour if they put their minds to it. Mohammed Ali probably could have been great at Kung Fu... as could have: Mikhail Barishnakov, Dan Gable, Chris Everet Lloyd, Wayne Gretsky, Michael Jordon, Nadia Komaniche, Pele, Walter Payton, and Elvis Stoijko (in fact, I think Elvis might be).

Late April, 2001 Cont'd

Today, I still feel like a warrior. A very, very, tired beaten-down one, but a warrior, nonetheless. Reading and conversation have deprived me of much needed sleep. Recuperation is a priority in a training regimen. Sometimes, however, the exuberance of renewal can make sleeping difficult.

I need sleep and proper nutrition. I have been neglectful in both these areas. For the next month, I will restrict my diet to rice, fish, lean chicken, fruits, vegetables and beer (hey, I'm not perfect).

I will also promise myself no reading after midnight. Funny, the books I can't seem to put down are books I've already read many times. The past few nights, I've focused on David Carradine's Spirit of Shaolin and Major Forrest E. Morgan's Living the Martial Way.

In rereading them, I am forced to realize that my book isn't necessary. Carradine and Morgan have already written books expressing the value of warrior philosophies. What's more, they've done it better than me. Still, when it comes to sharing insight, more is better.

If you haven't read these books read them. If you don't own them, buy them. They are manuals for life that should be read again and again... but buy my book first... I need the money more than they do.

An Honest Answer

Recently, I asked Mei-shen "Why do you want to study Kung Fu?" I ask this question of many students. There is a myriad of answers. Most are substantial, intelligent, even honest. One of the best responses is "Why not?" There are hundreds of reasons to study, but I can't think of one reason not to study.

Quite often our answers change. During one of my tests, Sifu asked me why I study now and also asked why I began. The answers I gave are no longer relevant.

I almost never began. Years ago, when I first looked into the martial art classes, I saw nothing of great interest to me. It was during this period that I was attacked in a downtown Windsor nightclub by a group of Americans. It may seem difficult to believe, but I did nothing to provoke them. As best I can figure, they were bored and looking for a game of "kick-the-canuck". I managed to drop two of them and the bouncers pulled away three or four others. Leaving a rather tall fellow squared off with me. He began throwing high crescent kicks at me (kicks I now recognize as sloppy). After I'd avoided two of them, I moved forward and grabbed the third kick, holding it above my head rendering him vulnerable to a high-impact takedown. A bouncer beat me to it. He football tackled my assailant to the floor.

My ignorance led me to believe this was a demonstration of the uselessness of martial arts. I failed to realize that my attacker, like most "martial artists," was a poor student. Months later, my friend, Dave convinced me to give Kung Fu a chance before condemning it. I went to the Wu Shen Temple (which carried the name <u>Shaolin Wu Te</u> at that time). I met Sifu and I was guided through my first class. I fell in love with it.

But none of this explains why I first wanted to study, and I doubt if any of the answers I gave in the past were truly on the mark.

Mei-shen enlightened me with her answer: "I just want to be interesting." Her answer has such purity. It was an honest expression of her humility, vanity, and desire. It wasn't until I thought about her words that it occurred to me this was the reason I began, so many years ago.

I study, now, as I will for life. I'm still in love with Kung Fu, every facet, every nuance. But, I began for the same simple reason... I just wanted to be interesting.

Sifu

Each time I practice one of the ancient routines of Kung Fu, it should be a dance that is focused yet mindless. Often it's not. It is difficult to guide myself through the traditional sets without wondering what criticism Sifu may have for me.

Sifu never graduated high school. I suppose if I tell you he is one of the wisest men I know, it would sound cliche. Have you met a martial artist who didn't think his mentor was wise? But Sifu is more than wise. He's absolutely Da Vincian.

On several subjects he is an expert; on others he simply knows a lot. What he hasn't set his hands too, he's read about.

His physical genius is obvious to all his students, though he rarely demonstrates forms or techniques himself. More often he prefers that our students represent the exemplary training at our school.

Within our temple walls, I've seen Sifu appear less than human; moving through forms with the agility of a squirrel, the grace of a crane, and the power of a tiger. He has leapt like a gazelle and pranced like a monkey.

He has thrown strikes at me with a speed that rivals lightning. And those strikes have landed as butterflies in a meadow.

When performing grappling techniques his limbs, his hands, his fingers possess the suppleness of snakes coiling in the proper fashion on instinct alone. Upon unleashing an application it is akin to any other masterful work of art; released with unsurpassed precision. I have grabbed Sifu about the wrist and felt my own hand weaken.

Sometimes, I believe Sifu to be a dragon casting himself in human form. I've met no one whom claims to have seen a dragon, so who is to say I'm wrong?

But Sifu's talents don't begin and end with the kinetic, spatial, or spiritual awareness needed within our school. His brilliance is furthered through his music. Sifu plays numerous instruments, at least: all styles of guitar, piano, drums, banjo, violin, xylophone, saxophone, flute, and harp. The truth is any instrument he hasn't played is just an instrument he hasn't picked up for a moment. It's the type of gift some are just born with.

Sifu sings, as well. When he sings a David Bowie song, he sounds just like Bowie. When he sings a Bruce Springsteen song, he sounds like Springsteen. When he sings a Mick Jagger song, he sounds like Jagger and when he sings a Burton Cummings song, he sounds like... well, not exactly Cummings, but close. That's pretty, damn good.

He's never been challenged by these musical attempts. In an effort to challenge himself, he composes. His work is in league with Bowie, Mercury, Zappa and Verdi.

He explores his visual artistry through Chinese calligraphy. He has informally studied scientific subject matter: nutrition, zoology, anatomy and biomechanics. He has an intuitive grasp of sociology and psychology. He is well-versed in European and Chinese history. He is an encyclopedia of knowledge in the three areas of most interest to him: Kung Fu, dogs and Rock n' Roll.

I once walked into our school and from across the room he asked me, "Jay, were you at the beach today?"

"Yes, Sifu," I answered.

"Oh, I thought I smelled sand."

Smelled sand?! He was across the room!

I don't believe he knows anything about brain surgery or rocket science, but it wouldn't surprise me if he did.

He balances pride and humility, humour and seriousness. He is a learned sage and a high school dropout. A partying rock-n'-roller from his early days, he, like me, has never touched an illegal substance. He is a spiritual philosopher, who watches *The Simpsons*. He has a bit of the outlaw in him, but he lives by a strict moral code. He is a man of paradox, and he isn't.

He is a dragon.

Early May, 2001

I sit in front of my residence again this evening with the intention of reading, but I am engaged in the activities of the pond. It has been a hot day, keeping the wildlife still. Now, as the night approaches and the air cools, the pond is reminiscent of a festival. In particular, the swallows come alive at dusk; soaring and diving like acrobats.

This area about my home contrasts the rest of my neighbourhood. Hsin Chuang is rather industrial, like Windsor, my hometown in Canada. The only plus is that it helps rid me of homesickness. I can simply walk by the manufacturers and listen to the machines and smell the lubricants and steel. I drift homeward and think, "Whew, I'm glad I'm not working there."

But, if you veer off the main road to a secondary road and from there head down an alley, you are suddenly back in time. There is a row of small, old shacks that pass for restaurants. In one of them, an old man sits and sleeps while his wife serves the guests. He wakes only occasionally to play a Taiwanese folk song on his yueqin (Chinese lute) before napping again.

Continuing past the restaurants you find gardens of fruits and flowers on both sides. The aroma greets you like a pleasant melody for the nose.

Between the gardens and my home is the pond I'm so fond of. Two days ago, the grassy shore and our pathway were swarmed by tiny toads smaller than the nail on my pinkie finger. The white crane that resides, here, had a feast that day. They are far too cute for my consumption, but I don't fault him for his nature.

The crane and I aren't the only frequenters of the pond. Often I share the shore with an old man. He sits, with his fishing pole, wearing clothes from a century ago, including a pointed farmer's hat. He could be a statue of a man for all the movement he makes. I suspect, for him, fishing is a form of meditation.

Mid-May, 2001

At a party two weeks ago, I consumed enough beer to bathe in. The following day I devoured a Big Mac meal in order to be functional again. Although it has virtually no nutritional value, a Big Mac meal is the supreme hangover remedy.

Aside from this momentary indulgence, I have adhered to my dietary agenda this past four weeks.

I'm toying with the notion of experimenting with some culinary strategies suggested by David Carradine, as prescribed by Vince Gironda. I prefer not call them diets, since Sifu Carradine implies they are more for spiritual alterations, rather than nutritional results. The best diet nutritionally is simply a responsible vegetarian (vegan or mollusk-inclusive). They're not for me. I border on carnivorous. If I watch live chicken run around, my mouth starts to water.

Yesterday's Playing Fields

I first began to understand the concepts of nutrition and physical fitness from my high school wrestling coach, Steve "Scam" Chamko. Among other things, Scam would repeat "Pintos run on low octane fuel, Mustangs run on high octane fuel." and "When you think you're ready to stop training today, ask yourself if your opponent has already gone home for the night."

Our team learned a lot from our coach; not only about how to be winners on the mats, but how to be winners in life.

It seems like a hundred years ago that we were the Sandwich Secondary Wrestling Team. But, if I let my memory flow, the emotion, the significant pride of belonging to that brotherhood comes back. Nothing in the world was more substantial to those teenage man-boys, than being a Sandwich Sabre. We learned the power of unity... that combining our energies increased our power not like simple addition, but exponentially. In 1987, we set out to be the best team in Ontario and instead became the best high school team in the whole damn country.

This is my book, so I'll take this opportunity to salute every canvas cowboy on that team from '83 to '88.   In particular: Jeff Phillips, Dan Murphy, Kam Lauzon, Luke and Donnie Collison, Randy and Rodney Levesque, Jimmy Joncus, Mean Gene Morone and, of course, the other four of the Fab Five: Jim (Mad Dog) MacDougall, Jim Meloche, Rodger Levesque (no sweat between our hands) and my sparring partner and dear friend, Ned (the Nightmare) Kalinovic.

I've saved someone for last. You may know Dave Beneteau as the 2nd place finalist in the U.F.C. Dave lost only to champions, Dan Severn and Oleg Taktarov (no shame there). Dave is an awesome fighter. He was also the Canadian Heavyweight Wrestling Champion.

I learned a great deal from Dave about how to be a champion by listening to him and even more by watching him. In high school, Dave seemed invincible. I was very surprised when he lost to a giant named Phil Portier.

As a true athletic champion, Dave focused himself on beating Portier. When the challenge arose, he didn't just beat him, he thrashed him and went on to become the Ontario champion that year.

This inspired me. I'd lost twice to a bruiser named Dennis Berrisford. Our first match was close. I'd lost by only three points. But, it shook me, because I'd never faced someone so vicious before. It was a bloodbath. We'd go out of bounds and he'd continue to come after me, crashing us to the tiles. At one moment, we'd both locked up for a throw and sent each other at least eight feet from the standing position. His cross-face was a literal strike to my face, drawing O+.

His goal was intimidation. It worked. The next time we faced off, he beat me easy.

A year and a half later, at the Ontario Championships, I was to face him again. The winner joined Team Ontario for the Nationals.

I reflected on Dave's victory and tried to evoke that same cocky attitude. I studied Berrisford in his last match and concluded, he was tough, but I was tougher.

Scam said only a few words, "Keep it at your pace!" This made sense. Berrisford moved about like the Tazmanian Devil in a Warner Brothers cartoon. So, I'd have to play it cool and smooth (like Bugs, I suppose).

Berrisford reared and shook like a crazed bull. But I barely moved.

He locked up like a gorilla trying to uproot a tree. I did a simple pummeling technique while popping my hips into him. He crashed landed outside the zone. 3 points.

The match had little variety after that. Again the bull met the matador. Boom 3 points. And again, Boom 3 points... and a pin. I jumped a mile high and landed into a Team Ontario jacket.

This is just another story of high school glory. But for many of us it is a playing field for life's future battles.

Dave and Scam taught me a great deal about emotional fortitude. They're just two of the many great teachers I've been blessed with throughout my tenure.

Teachers

If you've had any great teachers, please acknowledge them... aloud! Teachers and police officers suffer the same problem. When people discover their profession, they are usually hit with a "terrible cop" story or "I had this teacher once who I hated..." People seldom engage the conversation with "my favourite teacher was..." With this in mind, I dedicate this portion of the book to: Robert Warecki, Diane Schreoder, Brian Palenacki, Brian Raisebeck, Joe Tomc, Steve Chamko, Larry Carrick, Virgina Schimdt, Paul Ryan, Jackie Smyth, Edward A. Watson and Owen Klein.

In recounting the great teachers in my life, some bad examples may be necessary for contrast, but I hope the positive will out weigh the negative.

When I was in the 4th grade, I had a teacher with a mighty heart. His name was Mr. Warecki. At the end of the school year he announced he was leaving Anderdon Public. He wept.

Although, I was only nine years old, I understood that an injustice was taking place. The principal was pushing him out because of his continual conflicts with the Grade 5/ Music teacher. She was a mean and crabby witch. She was a mean and crabby witch with seniority.

Mr. Warecki had taught at other schools, and I hope he continued after he left us. He was good at it. But he was a young man then. Young men are prone to weakened egos. I hope he never doubted himself.

As for that grade 5 teacher, I hated her. She hated me. I insisted she was crazy.

For the first time that I can remember my mother took my opinion, over an adult's. After dealing with this woman for the first time, my mother agreed. There was definitely no reasoning with this woman.

A year ago, someone informed me that, almost 15 years after I had left that teacher's class, students, parents and teachers joined in protest to have her removed from her teaching position. Her obvious emotional disorder caused her to be cruel to her students. (Cruelty can be a real hindrance to an education.)

Another wonderful teacher of mine was Paul Ryan. He said, "If you want to be rich, ask a millionaire." Of course, he wasn't just talking about money. So many of us ask the opinions and advice of people who aren't qualified to answer.

If you want to know how to be a great teacher, ask Owen Klein. He is the greatest teacher I have ever known.

For the needed contrast, I will get the bad teacher story out of the way first:

Once in a science class, I raised my hand and dared to ask the teacher if he would go over a small portion of the lesson again. He said, "No."

"No?" I was confused, "Why not?"

"Are you paying attention?" he asked.

"I thought I was but I got the lost on that on those last steps of (I believe it was the break down of ATP in photosynthesis)."

"No, You're the only one, who missed it."

"You mean, I'm the only one with my hand up. Not everyone's as fast as Rob or Linda."

He was very nearly yelling, "Why should I go over this again for just one student?!"

As I picked up my books and made my way to the door, I exclaimed, "because that's what you get paid 40 grand a year to do!"

I was never reprimanded for this. Maybe somebody decided I was justified, maybe even the science teacher himself. After all, its not as though I was a punk in the habit of sounding off to my teachers.

You see, I struggled in that class -which was all the more reason to help me when I asked. I would have accepted, "Come see me after school," but I wasn't given that option. It doesn't take a good teacher to get through to the gifted students. Anyone can teach them. Sometimes they can even teach themselves. A good teacher can get through to the drowning scholar.

Owen Klein gets through to his students because he's on their side. There is no 'you against me' attitude in his lessons. On the contrary, he reveals everything to his pupils, as though each was a close friend. Prior to examinations, he divulges the questions... I kid you not. Owen knows something many students are unaware of; he remembers something many teachers have forgotten; it is not the teacher's job to trick the students. The goal should be that the student learns the material. Why should a student have to guess what is the content of that material? As Owen said, "I just want you to know more when you leave, than when you came in."

I hold fast to the belief that teaching is one of the noble professions. Teach, heal, protect, provide or save! If you're not doing one of these things, you're not contributing.

I recently discovered something distressing about the old musician at the restaurant I mentioned earlier. He works.

The other day I stopped in for chicken and rice and saw him cooking and cleaning. I'd thought only his wife worked. I had to inform him of my disappointment. Prior to that day, he was my newest hero.

Earlier I mentioned that I was the North American Shuai-Chiao Champion in the year 2000. I trust you weren't impressed. It seems every time you turn around, you bump into somebody who is the champion of something. If so, take a moment and congratulate that person on their laurels. He/she no doubt worked hard for them. Just don't ever be intimidated by them.

If you are champion, take a moment, right now and congratulate yourself... even if it was fifty years ago.

You can always tell how pathetic someone's life is by how far back they have to go to recapture glory... 'Well, I remember... when I was... a sperm... it was the day of the big race... thousands of us entered...

- Jim Carrey

Hey, we've all won at least one race.

Regardless, of the "it's not whether you win or lose" philosophy, winning feels great. Losing seldom feels even bearable. We are supposed to be consoled by the fact that losing is such an education. Rarely, does that help. But I do recall a moment in time when I was more than content with it.

In my youth, I was to face Canada's Olympian, Lawrence Holmes at an open wrestling tournament. He was much more experienced than me, but I was confident. Not that I would beat him, but that I would give him a real fight for it.

One minute into the match, I had scored a point, and Holmes had been cautioned for passivity (unwillingness to fight). He'd evened the score at one to one, but was unable to turn me with his gut-wrench. I felt world-class.

Thirty seconds later the match was over. Holmes had found a way to tilt me, and proceeded to do so eight times. A fifteen-point advantage is a mercy ruling and the match is stopped.

I never had a chance. I wasn't emotionally mature enough at that time to defeat someone at that level. But there was no humiliation, nor remorse. At 19, I'd scored on an Olympic veteran. I consider it one of the best matches of my wrestling career.

Nevertheless, given the choice between winning or losing and learning, like most people, I'd sooner win and learn nothing.

The celebration is sweeter.

Tao Te Ching

The skeleton of the story is this:

Sometime after 551 B.C., in the hamlet Chu Jen, in the province of Chu, lived Li Erh. He would later be well known under the name acquired from his community, Lao Tzu (the elder).

Lao Tzu did not create the Tao.

Much like his younger contemporary, Confucius, Lao Tzu was well respected as a teacher/philosopher. Even Confucius, himself, sought out Lao Tzu's wisdom.

Near the end of his life, Lao Tzu left his home to find solitude. As he was to exit the kingdom, a soldier guarding the pass recognized the sage and begged him, first to write down his philosophy for posterity, before disassociating himself from humanity.

Some stories describe this encounter rather like blackmail. In these versions, the keeper of the pass refuses Lao Tzu passage until he agrees to write. In any account, the sage sits down and writes two books: <u>Tao Ching</u> and <u>Te Ching</u>, today compiled together under the title <u>Tao Te Ching</u>.

Lao Tzu did not create the Tao.

Lao Tzu's book of semi-poetic prose outlines the concept of acceptance with the world. It is living in a manner that is simply in accordance with nature, without conflict or contention. It is flowing; riding the waves of life much like a cork.

All beings, save human, live in this manner. They give it no name, for it requires no thought. It just is. Lao Tzu most keenly observed this and hesitantly gave it a name for the sake of our systematic brains. That name is Tao (the way).

The Tao is most often symbolized by the Yin-Yang. Yin Yang represents two complete opposites in balance, as a harmonious fact of nature. Even this is misleading, for what we deem as opposites can't really exist without each other and don't really exist as opposing forces, but as joined relations.

Yin is representative of the cold, dark, feminine side; Yang, the warm, light masculine side. There are nearly infinite connections: hard/soft, day/night, wind/earth, fire/water, hunger/contentment, humour/seriousness, movement/stagnation, etc.

Some have considered this a symbol a portrait of good and evil: the Yang being goodness, and the dark, feminine Yin representing evil. I'm tempted to agree, but I cannot.

Where does evil exist in nature? If a wolf kills a rabbit, is she evil? No, she is only hungry. How about the evil rabbit that out runs the wolf depriving her of sustenance? - ridiculous.

It has been said that the Tao transcends morality; but rather it never aspires to it... fortunately.

       *   *   *

It seems to me that people of the past, particularly the working class, required systems of worship to make their lives meaningful. Like many great concepts of the world, for better or worse, Taoism evolved into a religion. Borrowing from the pantheons of earlier religions, rituals were formed and temples were built.

Am I a Taoist? Some would say 'no', as I do not ascribe to the dogma of the religion. But what is natural about worship?

When I hunger, I eat. When I thirst, I drink. When I tire, I sleep. This is in accordance with the Tao. Which category I fall in doesn't concern me.

> *This is*
> *the greatest poem*
> *ever written*
> *on understanding*
> *the Tao.*

- Jay McCoy

Meditation

The most common objective of meditation is to empty the mind completely. This is not always possible for all of us. It becomes more obtainable through practice. In the years since I began meditation, I have only obtained this state of absolute emptiness, devoid of words or picture or colour, about three times. However, even to rid your mind of most thoughts for a prolonged period of time is helpful in relieving stress, feeling rested and thinking clearly.

I have experimented with several different methods, which I believe is but a fraction of the techniques throughout the world. You can try sitting in the lotus position, i.e., legs crossed, back straight, shoulders rounded and wrist resting on the knees or in the lap, with middle fingers touching the thumbs. This was my preferred position for years.

More recently, I prefer to be on my back with my feet flat on the floor, as I now, trust myself not to fall asleep. I'll probably return to the lotus position, but for moment, I'm choosing to experiment. Experimenting is good, but only after you have given one method a sincere try. Research postures with a credible teacher. There is a connection between mind, body and spirit (in truth it is more than just a connection). Proper bodily postures suitably align the spiritual channels.

Before getting the mind completely empty, get somewhere close. Think only of one thing. I have used my breathing as a tool, focusing only on the natural rhythm. On occasion, I've consciously slowed my breathing and heartbeat. As I improve, I may not have to "consciously" do anything.

I've tried repeating a single word or sound aloud over and over again. The purpose is to use it to push out all other thoughts. Eventually, the practitioner stops using this syllable aloud and simply continues the rhythm from within, then, gradually that slips away, as well. Many people have had more success with this method than have I.

What works best for me is to picture only white. At the beginning, I may need to repeat to myself, over and over "white paper, white paper" before the image is secure enough. Thoughts sneak in, but I don't dwell on them. I just dismiss them. Eventually there is only me and the whiteness. And if I'm very lucky, even that leaves me and there is nothingness.

Usually, it is the sudden realization that I've achieved nothingness that shatters it. For a long time, I believed I had achieved this state for only a fraction of second. It has since occurred to me that in this state, time would not be ascertainable, so I really don't know how long I was there. I do know that after checking the clock, sometimes what I believed to be an hour long session was closer to two hours.

Some people prefer to focus their thoughts on colours (I've used yellow to brighten my mood). It is believed by some that purple allows you to separate your astral self from your corporal form. Do not use black. Black is a canvas for the mind. Conjuring images will be inevitable. If your intent is to use meditation as an instrument for physical healing, colour is essential. But that's someone else's book.

Don't close your eyes. Contrary to what you may have heard or read, closing your eyes isn't helpful. You wouldn't be expected to close your ears or nose, nor shut off your sense of touch. Your senses are still existent during meditation; you simply aren't allowing them to distract you. It's not the trance-like state as it is often depicted. That leads to sleep - which is not the goal. Don't close your eyes.

Koans are a popular Asian tool. They are a paradoxical and/or profound thought on which to dwell. Some people call them riddles, but riddles are meant to be solved. Koans are not. I prefer to think of them as tests in simplicity. If that is unclear to you, just "listen for the sound of one hand clapping," and it should reveal itself.

A former boss of mine, Ron Brough has suggested techniques that I've enjoyed. Ron is not a manufacturing quality manager. Yes, that's his job, but Ron is not someone to define himself by his occupation.

Ron began his spiritual awakening years ago as he began to explore his native Canadian heritage. He showed me the value of instrumental music, as a tool of meditation. I don't mean soft background music, as you might suspect. Ron's prescription was to have the volume up so loud your mind swam in it, washing away most other thoughts. I've tried this with European classical, Chinese classical, and Heavy Metal (though it has vocals). Beethoven's 9th and Nazareth's Greatest Hit's rejuvenated me. Mozart's Eine Kleine Nacht Muzic, Chinese Classical, and Enya melted me.

Ron provided me with a short list of questions to be asked if I was using meditation conquer inner-strife:

1: What is the biggest problem I am facing, right now?
2: Have I faced this problem before?
3: How would my father handle this problem?
4: How would my mother handle this problem?
5: How will I handle this problem?

These sound like common sense questions to dealing with a problem, but funny thing about common sense... not so common.

I don't know the sources of Ron's prescriptions. They could be Aboriginal North American or Slavic gypsy. Ron's pretty multi-faceted.

Regarding all this meditation, is the pragmatist in your head arguing with the believer in your heart? Does reaching a higher level of consciousness sound like a lot of hocus-pocus? All right, here's the scientific nitty-gritty on how it works:

I've always believed that human intelligence was a gift, just like a wing or a fang. But it is also a curse. The human brain is a busy instrument. It is capable of millions of simultaneous synaptic connections.

The superior parietal lobe area of the brain is flooded with information regarding time and space. In particular, it defines our conception of our physical being. It tells us we have a body and where that body is. During mediation, we block sensory input to the parietal lobe. Hence, the brain ceases to distinguish between what is "self" and what is not; ergo, achieving the "one with the universe" effect. The feeling is euphoric.

Meditation isn't the only way to achieve it. Many have done so without any attempt - simply getting lost in a sunset, or watching a baby play.

Sometimes, rather than emptying the mind, a sensory overload can cause the hippocampus portion of the brain to act as a control valve, retarding the flow of impulses to the neurons. This creates a similar effect of losing your sense of self and, instead, feeling connected to everything and everyone around.

You may have seen someone in part of a religious sermon or ritual, whom becomes crazed with euphoria. Chanting, dancing and other common parts of religious ritual are powerful stimuli, particularly when coupled with symbols that have strong emotional significance to the believer. But a Rolling Stone concert can have the same affect. Hundreds of fans can melt their identities and merge.

The most common experience of this sensory overload is intense sex. During the height of arousal, often any sense of when, where, or even who we are, is lost.

You already know that sex, in a safe, monogamous relationship is healthy for the body. Now, you can appreciate the healing it can have for the mind and spirit...**as if you needed another reason to have sex!**

*   *   *

"To know one's true mind, he must first banish all thought from it."
- St. Nilus

In one form or another, meditation has existed in all religions and philosophies. The yogis of the Hindu Bhakti may be the most famous for the use of meditation, but Aboriginal North Americans in their seat lodges experience a form of meditation, as do Christian monks in solitude practice "contemplation" as decreed by Benedict and Augustine.

Within the doctrine of Sufism, the profit Mohammed describes the evocation of the name of God as a polishing of the heart.

"There is but one god and his name is Allah."
The repetition of this "zikr" can be done as part of a group ritual or in solitude. It begins out loud and gradually softens as it is internalized. The Sufi know that when the heart begins, the mouth may stop.

Kabbalist Jews are aware of a hierarchy of planes of existence ascending to heaven. The lowest level, Yesod, being that of the unenlightened human mind, is where most of us dwell. The Metatron, chief of angels, teacher of humans and voice of God (as we are ill-equipped to survive God's voice) sits at the highest level. Through meditation the Kabbalist Jews seek to reach a higher level. They look inside themselves for a place above their ego, Tiferet, the bridge between planes of enlightenment. They are but temporary glimpses. But the hope is that with enough devotion the effect will be a permanent welcoming to the next plane.

If your interest is piqued, a detailed study in any religion via its books and clergy will reveal much more than I can provide you.

Regarding Religion

If you consider yourself a religious person, for God's sake (or rather for the sake of your relationship with God), look into it. Too often, alleged devotees are ignorant of their own religions.

A couple of years ago, I was distributing flyers for our Kung Fu school throughout my hometown. The lady at the Christian bookstore rejected the idea of putting a flyer on their bulletin board, stating "the martial arts are in conflict with Christianity." Hmmm.

You will never hear me complain about the layout of the instrument panel in DC-9 aircraft. Do you know why? ...**Because I don't know**

anything about flying planes. Why do people without experience try to tell us what the martial arts are about?

My perplexed smile must have suggested I wanted more of an explanation, because she continued, "it's the whole meditative aspect that we're against."

I returned to her three days later with a compilation of writings. Some were my own thoughts, others were essays from Christian clergy, who were also martial artists, the rest were scripture from the Bible. When I presented it to her, I was quick to assure her it was not my intention to spur an argument. I only hoped she would read it and perhaps gain some new perspective. She surprised me with her willingness.

Peace; passivity or responsibility

I recall the lady had made a reference to the martial arts being different from the passivity expressed by Jesus. Is this the same Jesus, who went to the temple with a whip in his hand and starting kicking over tables? Which Bible was she reading? The Bible is fraught with examples of warriorship. The most remembered is when David smote Goliath ('smote' is a great word, isn't it?) There are the stories of the Gideons, Joshua, Samson, and Simon Peter, whose sword separated a soldier's ear from his head, in defense of Christ.

I consider myself to be peaceful, internally and externally. Passivity has its place, but passivity can be detrimental to inner-peace. Good people, particularly warriors, need to take arms against injustice.

"All that evil needs to succeed is for good men to sit and do nothing."
- Judeo-Christian adage

"With great power comes great responsibility."
- Spider-man
(as dictated by Stan Lee)

The differences in religions can be interesting, but I also find the commonalities quite intriguing. The "Golden Rule" seems to be an element, which is inherent of every spiritual system I've examined, "Do unto others as you would have them do unto you."

A little something for men to consider:

Another coincidence of spiritual literature is the perspective of women.
The Torah/Old testament shared by Jews and Christians tells of Eve impairing Adam's judgment, of Delilah's betrayal of Samson, and of Jezebel's seductive power. Many Muslims accept the belief that a woman's power to tempt should be arrested by the coverings of long clothes and veils. The Hindu are warned by their scripture to avoid women, wealth and non-believers. The Taoist Yin-Yang symbol describes the feminine side as dark, mysterious and cold.

Is there some great spiritual insight to be seen, here? Does God/Allah/Jehovah/Fate/Nature have something to tell us?

Smart women will point out that these scriptures and doctrines were the words of God, *only as perceived and defined by men*...that's just what they want us to believe...

Differences

You would think with important similarities there would be little need for separation, but it does occur in Western religions. A person cannot really be both a Baptist and a Jew, nor Catholic and a Jehovah's Witness. But Eastern religions do not exclude each other. Even Confucism and Taoism, which appear to be in juxtaposition, are woven together in the daily lives of millions of Chinese.

The other day, at the near by university campus, I saw a lady Buddhist monk engage in conversation with a Catholic nun. To me this was a unique and fascinating picture. But it would be feasible to hold fast to both Catholic and Buddhist principles. It brings to mind the story of the Buddhist monk, who having read the words of Jesus, said, "He was indeed a Buddha." Such concepts are comforting if one keeps an open mind. Alas, not everyone does.

There are phrases people use in reference to the devotedly religious, sometimes, "religious fanatic" or "Jesus freak." I try to avoid these labels, as they seem to imply some sort of disorder. (Actually truly devoted martial artists get similar labels.) I believe having made a spiritual choice, people should be fully faithful to this lifestyle; otherwise, there is no point.

When Jehovah's Witnesses or Sister's of the Church of the Latter Day Saint's arrive on our doorsteps some of us respond with indignation. Why? If their beliefs don't suit you, kindly send them on their way. It's no skin of their nose. Their mission was to try.

The people that disturb me are those that condemn others for their beliefs. On the night I left Canada for Taiwan, I sat with a missionary in the Toronto airport. She was bound for Hawaii to visit a friend. We talked of her travels and mine. As well, she spoke of her beliefs with great enthusiasm.

The conversation was quite pleasant until I informed her that I'm not Christian. Without bothering to ask my beliefs, she said, "Oh, it always makes me so sad... when I travel I meet some wonderful people but I know they I will not see them in the kingdom of heaven because they haven't accepted Jesus as their lord."

I responded, "But they're wonderful people, if they're good to others...?" She interrupted my question, "if we could all find our own way into heaven, Jesus wouldn't have had to die for our sins, would he?!"

In just a couple of sentences, she had managed to insult, at least 75% of the world's population. According to her, every Jew, Muslim, Hindu Taoist, Totemist, Buddhist, Agnostic, etc., despite the purity of their actions, is eternally damned. The Dalai Lama, himself, will rot in hell, because he hasn't accepted Jesus as his saviour.

Fanatic [n.] 1. a person whose enthusiasm for something, esp. a political or religious cause, is extreme to the extent that it blinds judgment.

I could have exploded with harsh words, but I chose instead to turn the other cheek. I thanked her for sharing and politely excused myself.

*   *   *

By now some theologians are exclaiming, "No Muslim, Jew or Christian could really embrace a second religion with a pantheon of gods, since they know there is only one God to be worshipped." This is only a contradiction if one misinterprets the alleged 'pantheon of gods." 'Gods' is a misnomer, one that has been carried on for centuries, since someone translated the Chinese word 'shun' into deity. Subsequently, it became synonymous with worshipped. In fact, the Chinese don't worship these figures in the way God is worshipped. A more accurate translation would be 'saint'. One prays to Mazu for safe travel, just as one prays to St. Christopher. General Gwan is the patron of friendship, as he was so loyal to his friends. Gwan was a warrior and a true friend; how not unlike St. Simon

Peter. They were real people who have been canonized since their deaths. They are not supposed to have contributed to the creation of our existence.

There may be those who still worship P'an Ku as the creator. Although, the stories vary all over the world, the understanding of the will of the creator is the same, whether the name is P'an Ku, Allah, Jehovah, Ralph or Betty.

I'd like to begin the petition here to rectify the misinterpretation, by changing the translation of 'shun' in every text or dictionary from 'god' to 'saint'. It sounds like a small detail, but I think the ramifications might be grand. Perhaps a greater sharing in spirituality would result. Probably not.

Late May, 2001

I am Jay McCoy of the Northern Shaolin Seven Star Praying Mantis Style Kung Fu lineage; chosen defender of the Wu Shen Temple, 9th Generation from the Shaolin Temple in Shangtung.

Yeah, I'm braggin'.

You won't hear me brag about my own abilities (at least, not sober), but I'm quick to expound on the excellence of our school, and how we have adhered to tradition. We have not lost our sense of the value of the history that begets our training.

In 1664 the Ming Dynasty fell to the Manchurians. Wu Xan Kwei convinced the Manchu military to aid him in overthrowing the government. He didn't count on the Manchurians' decision to keep China for themselves, thus beginning the Ching Dynasty.

Whether or not the Manchu had any right to claim China, they excelled in cultural and artistic development. Great literature, such as The Dream of the Red Chamber (considered one of China's best novels) was written. Paintings, sculptures, carvings, workings in metal continued to become more detailed. And, though outlawed for common citizens, the martial arts still flourished and evolved.

Prior to the invasion, when it was still legal to practice martial arts, a man named Wong Long wandered China testing his prowess in friendly combat. He was an excellent swordsman and a highly proficient tiger stylist. Nevertheless, he was constantly reminded that his kung fu was second only to the Shaolin monks. In 1664, determined to prove himself, Wong Long went to the Shaolin Temple in Shangtung. He challenged the monks there to sparring. They tried to deny him, but he was persistent. Finally, a match was set between Wong Long and a novice. Wong Long was defeated.

Wong Long did not run off like a dog with his tail between his legs. He stepped up his training. At some point, Wong Long, himself, became a monk at the temple, training with others on the temple grounds, and on his own in the woods outside the temple walls. When in his story this occurred is a matter of conjecture. Some historians say that Wong Long was a monk long before this incident. In any case, after a few months, Wong Long again issued his challenge. This time he bested all his brothers... all, but one, his senior brother continued to beat Wong Long every time they contested.

Although Wong Long developed a close bond of friendship with his senior brother, he never rid himself of his desire to defeat him.

One day, while meditating outside the temple walls, Wong Long heard the shrill shriek of a cicada. He looked to see a cicada engaged in battle with a praying mantis. The skinny little mantis was being pressed down by the goliath-like bug. To Wong Long's surprise, the mantis suddenly pivoted his head, twisted his limbs and turned the cicada to its back. Then the mantis proceeded to devour it, in a ghoulish manner.

So impressed was Wong Long by the praying mantis, he scooped it up and spent months studying it. He poked and prodded it with grass and sticks and mimicked its movements.

Wong Long used his newfound techniques to finally thwart his brother. His brother, now abbot of the temple, asked Wong Long to begin a system based on his new knowledge. He began by creating the form Bung Bo. From there, other experienced monks of various systems aided in the development of Praying Mantis.

Of course, the footwork of a four-legged mantis is impossible to copy. Therefore Wong Long included the footwork of a monkey. I've been told by people that he borrowed from the Monkey system. This is the wrong assumption. The Monkey system was developed, after Praying Mantis by Kau See in 1842. Within, Shaolin were white gibbon techniques that were included in the Mantis systems; this may have included much of the footwork.

Both Mantis and Monkey, as well as, Eagle claw are considered to be advanced schools. They were not developed in the Henan temple as were most animal styles. They came later and each was the product of collaboration between experienced stylists of other systems, who contributed their most advanced techniques. Many hybrid schools won't teach Mantis, Monkey, nor Eagle forms until a student has learned another system in its entirety. Certainly, there are other advanced systems. The numbers of such systems are few, but the numbers of practitioners who claim to be studying an advanced system are many.

Praying Mantis is an obscure art, despite its numerous branches: Six Harmony, Yin Yang, Bare, Speckled-back, Eight Step, Tai-mantis, etc. The original system is Seven Star, aptly named by Wong Long for his hope that it would spread as far on earth as those who can see the constellation, Ursa Major.

This is my system. I have investigated numerous martial arts. I've studied a few, briefly; mostly kung fu systems: Wing Chun, Hung Gar, Tien

Shen Pai and Tiger Claw, but I have chosen Praying Mantis as my path, because it is the best system in the world... for me.

Everyone believes his or her system is the best... and everyone is right. But not as right as me.

Along with Praying Mantis, I study Chin Na. This grappling art of no discernable origin is a system in and of itself. However, as it developed gradually over the decades, along side other Shaolin systems, it is generally a supplement to all others styles.

It is not possible to know how many monks within Shaolin temple worked on and studied the Seven Star Mantis system, but it was Shen Shao Dow Ren who first brought it outside the temple.

My lineage proceeds from there:

1: Shen Shao Dow Ren
2: Li San Chen
3: Wong Rong Sung
4: Fan Yu Tang (the legendary Da Fan)
5: Lin Ching Shan
6: Wang Tsung Ching
7: Wu Heng Li
8: Simon Pszczonak
9: Jay McCoy

Rain

I had wanted to keep every journal entry upbeat. Each one should be a testament to how my life has become blissful since my alleged revelation (to reconnect with the shaolin philosophies). So far, that's been easy. I've had some frustrating moments, but overall, I've suffered very little culture shock.

Taiwanese people more closely resemble Canadians than the Japanese. In Japan, my second and third months were fraught with culture shock. But here, I'm usually quite happy.

Today is a downer. It's a day of non-stop, heavy rain. My mood is easily affected by the conditions of nature. I don't sleep during the full moon. In fact, I get antsy... sometimes rowdy. On a sunny day I may cartwheel like a child. And heavy rain brings me down.

I've failed at three attempts to train, today. I won't push it anymore. Sometimes, it is best to let it be.

It doesn't help that Mei-shen is at her parent's house in Taipei city because she is sick again. That's three times in one month. She hasn't followed my health advice, but perhaps she'll listen to her doctor. She hasn't called yet to inform me of what he's said, so I worry.

I believe all she needs to do is to replace her salty diet with something healthier and do more training. But that's a circle; she can't practice Kung Fu if she's sick and she can't feel completely healthy without exercise. At least, if she's sick in bed, today's the day to do it. Being sick on beautiful day when you should be outside makes you feel that much worse. I hope she appreciates the timing of her illness.

I already feel better... writing has that effect, but there's an additional factor, too. Just outside my window I heard a young couple laughing. It brought to mind days when I've been caught in warm summer rain and had fun with it. You know, those days when you've gotten so soaked there's no point in running for shelter. And you just let go. Maybe I'll go outside and pretend it happened by accident.

*   *   *

"What a bad idea!" I exclaimed aloud, even though I was alone. It's late may in Taiwan, so naturally the air is sub-tropical warm, but let me tell ya', that rain was Yukon cold.

I was determined to stand in the rain until I grew accustomed to it. After a few minutes I began to laugh out loud at my own stupidity. And then it happened. I still felt the cold wetness, but I accepted it. More than that, I liked it. I was a part of it. It inspired me, and I had a fabulous Kung Fu workout in the short grass by the pond.

If I didn't have to work this afternoon, I'd still be there, in the downpour, dancing and smiling.

I hope it rains again tomorrow.

Late May, 2001

I had a dream, this morning. "Past the wit of man to say what dream it was... man is but an ass..." or at least this man was an ass.

My mind returned to a time when I just discovered my ex's infidelity. In my dream, however, I handled it with less dignity. I confronted her with great hostility. All the while, my mind occasionally replaced her with my old high school flame, Cherie. Of course at the time of the dream I was unaware of the change.

I thought it strange to happen, now. I haven't had this sort of dream in over three months. Six months ago, they happened every night and I would always wake up angry. Not today, though. This morning I was peaceful.

I think I finally realized what my mind has been trying to tell me. The dreams hadn't made sense replacing her with Cherie. Cherie was never unfaithful. She couldn't be; it's the very antithesis of who she is. I believe my brain wants to remind me that there are still women who are pure of heart.

Cherie stopped by to see me with her new baby, just two days before I left for Taiwan. This visit was a surprise since we stopped really being friends five years ago. Her husband, who was just her boyfriend at the time, wasn't comfortable with our friendship. He wasn't comfortable with her relationship with any of her male friends.

For a long time, I resented him for that. After all, it didn't make sense not to trust Cherie. If I thought she was capable of cheating on him, it would break **my** heart. But I judged him too harshly. I don't know his past experiences with women. Now, I think I understand him better... maybe we've walked a mile in similar moccasins.

Before Cherie left, I thanked her. Though we hadn't spoken in so long, the memory of who she is helped to heal me. She is one of the few reminders I have that decent women of moral stamina exist in the world. Somewhere beneath my bitterness, I was hoping my journals would take this turn for the better. Still, it's always two steps forward and one step back; but waking this morning with only serenity inside me, that's one really big step forward.

I generally don't like love poems; however, this I wrote many years ago, as a gift for Cherie:

Girl of Green Gone

Girl of green gone
pushing me forward,
to face the giants,
to be a giant.
You make less of the challenge
by allowing me two worlds.
Though the steel land of the aged
is all around me,
I still see the emerald city
in your eyes.

A Little Homesick

It started last night, wishing one of the boys was with me having a beer. I was thinking how much I missed just sitting front of the T.V. with Rich watching sitcoms. I was aching to be at some pub back home singing folk songs with Kevin and Brad. I miss Grand Bend where we'd spend our long weekends in the summer, playing all day and just sitting beneath the stars all night. We'd joke, sing and sometimes get philosophical. I remember quite often hoping that every summer would be like the one I was having. Many of them were... each the same repetition of happiness.

I suspect more are to come. But for now, I look forward to a different kind of happiness; at least for a while.

Early June, 2001

The Portuguese named this island "Formosa," which means beautiful. It's simple, but appropriate. In less than 32300 km^2 is a collage of lush sub-tropical forest, fertile plains, and regal mountains rising from the sea like Neptune's trident. My eyes have again been blessed by my travels.

I've often been asked what is the most beautiful thing I've ever seen:

I've stood on a mountain on Ios, seeing a sun-baked cliff stand guard over a white beach that stretched into an endless azure sea. All framed in a powder blue... a cloudless, powder blue. I stood there long enough to see this blue darken with the approaching night until it became indigo, seasoned with sparks of silver. Stationary sparks which contrasted their rolling, tumbling reflections below.

And this was not the most beautiful thing I've ever seen.

I've sat on the sandy shore of the Atlantic Ocean in Florida and watched the sunrise. Pink and pale yellow softened the dark horizon... expanding gradually, as they changed to bright yellow and red. Until the centre of it all burst open with bright orange.

I've seen these same pinks, yellows, reds and oranges splashed along the wilderness that blankets the hills on the north side of the St. John River in autumn in New Brunswick.

And neither of these were the most beautiful thing I've ever seen.

I've stood before Da Vinci's <u>Mona Lisa</u> at the Louvre in Paris, France; lay beneath the cherry blossoms at an O-Hanami festival in Tohoku, Japan... I've watched as a newborn baby grasped the index finger of my right hand... and with that same hand I've fed wild dear and smaller creatures of the woods.

And none of these were the most beautiful thing I've ever seen.

Mid- June, 2001

My family and friends haven't written lately. I'm unsure about how this relationship with Mei-shen is unfolding. I have financial troubles. I've been sick this week. But what's set me off the most? The gym is closed. This day sucks... But heck, its only 12:30, there's lots of time for it to get better.

Some guy named Cedric just called the radio station and requested that they play the saddest song they could find. The D.J. jokes about Cedric wanting to bring the whole island down with him, but agrees to find the saddest song during the commercial break.

My mind searched for what might be the saddest song. At first, I think of Travis Tritt's *Tell Me I Was Dreaming*, but that takes second place to Diamond Rio's *You're Gone*. But there's no country station in Taiwan, so I was certain that I wouldn't hear it. I was shocked to discover the (possibly psychic) D.J. is also a fan of *You're Gone*.

The last time I heard this song, it was an echo of my pain. Now, I remember, how every day for months, I would look in the mirror and force myself to repeat, "Your life will get better, your life will get better, your life will get better." I was right.

My worst days here are better than the best days I was having this past winter. And should truly bad days come again, I'll ride them out their conclusion. And be happy that I can be happy without needing reasons to be happy.

Am I important?
When I snap my fingers,
the universe changes.

When a mouse farts,
the universe changes.

A Cold Beer for the Soul

Dear Mr. Canfield,

I am familiar with your series of books which began with <u>Chicken Soup for the Soul</u>. A friend of mine once criticized your books as corny, but I like them. To read through anyone of them and not find at least one story you've enjoyed, you'd have to be... well, soulless.

I wonder if you'd be interested in a different kind of story. Mine is not written by someone who has recovered thanks to some celestial intervention. I'm still in a dark place.

I feel as though I've lost so much of myself to heartache and humiliation. I don't recognize myself anymore. This pit of depression seems inescapable... but I know it is not.

I've read many of the stories you've compiled. While they were enjoyable at happier times in my life, now they seem meaningless. I'm not writing to criticize. I'm writing to offer your readers another perspective; the perspective of someone whose still there in the darkness.

I will get better. *I will rebuild my life. I will be happy again.*

I will do this by digging inside myself for my strength. Unlike most of your stories, I have no inspiring act of nature to motivate me nor words from unlikely sages nor any whisper of angels in my ear.

Sometimes, it's entirely up to us to do it ourselves. We can't sit and wait for some divine intervention to give us a sign.

Please print my letter. Maybe somebody will be reading your next book looking for some miracle, when what he really needs is to get off his butt and make it happen... like me.

Sincerely,

Jay McCoy

It's kind of old school thinking. My father's generation didn't rely on therapists and support groups. They didn't whine on T.V. talk shows. They didn't look to shift responsibility or want for pity. It's that "pull yourself up by your own bootstraps" mentality that got me through.

I went to work, I trained in Kung Fu, and, instead of some support group, I went out with my pals and discussed life over a nice, cold beer. That's what my soul needed more than chicken soup.

I didn't say I was unimportant.

I, also, didn't say the mouse was unimportant.

June 14, 2001

Small earthquake today. That added a little fun to the morning.

Chinese Medicine

I worked for a man, who suffered severe neck pains. He took pills, he used some device around his neck when he slept, and he had regular visits to the chiropractor. I suggested he try acupuncture. His response was, "I tried it once. Chinese medicine doesn't work for me."

Do people listen to themselves when they speak? After months of western medicinal methods had failed him, he said, "I tried it **once**..." and then he gave up on Chinese medicine. Ironically, he's Chinese.

Mei-shen, too, has said that Chinese medicine doesn't work on her. She sticks to Western techniques. However, she's sick more than anybody I know.

In contrast, my co-worker, Brian is a firm believer in the Chinese methodology. Brian is a big, rough, lovable South African with a great sense of humour. Two days ago, at 7:30 in the morning, Brian was stopped at a red light on his motor scooter. He was hit by a drunk driver (yes, I said 7:30 in the morning). Brian was thrown about ten metres from the vehicle. When he awoke with the police and ambulance attendants around him, he couldn't move his legs. You can imagine his fear.

At the hospital, following a diagnosis, the doctor had Brian lain on his stomach. He tapped a single needle into Brian's neck and proceeded to swing his legs horizontally. An hour later, Brian was up and about, as though nothing happened.

Chinese medicine is not focused solely on healing, but on prevention as well. Maintaining good health can be achieved through Asian techniques which strengthen the internal energies, such as: meditation, yoga, Tai Chi, Chi Gung, Falun Dafa, and, of course, the martial arts.

The doctors of Chinese medicine also recommend Feng Shuai, which is a system, both spiritual and scientific. This system of design involves the positioning of all things in your life, which are perceived by the five senses, in a manner that provides harmony.

The one preventative measure common to both Eastern and Western medicine is life-style. By life-style, I refer to nutrition, exercise, sleep patterns, and the avoidance of toxins. Today, we consider this common sense. As I've said before, funny thing about common sense - it's not so common.

There are five basic strands of healing in Chinese medicine: herbalism, moxabustion, cupping, acupuncture and acupressure. My knowledge of these methods ranges from very little to nothing at all.

What I do know is that Chinese medicine is a more holistic approach than Western medicine, which has a reductionist approach. It doesn't isolate a problem, but rather sees the problem as a system of disharmony of the whole body. The body's Yin qualities are not in balance with its Yang qualities. For example, any organ or part of the body may be experiencing heat or cold excess or deficiency. This may be caused by an external force, such as, weather or flood or the root may be internal. Poor anger control management can result in excessive heat in the liver, which can lead to a stroke.

This example I've taken from Tom Williams' book, <u>The Complete Illustrated Guide to Chinese Medicine; A Comprehensive System for Health and Fitness</u> 1. It is everything its title suggests and it is the best book I've ever read for introducing Chinese medicine to novices like myself.

My first experience with the healing aspect of Chinese medicine involved acupuncture and acupressure. These usually work in conjunction with each other. I had suffered a boxer's break in my right hand (which was really just a sprain) and I had strained my wrist and elbow.

I went to see Dr. James Zheng on Ouellette Ave. in Windsor. One session was all that was needed to make my arm as good as new. It seemed to me to be a miracle. Since then, no acupuncture session has produced such immediate results in relieving my injuries. However, I have always felt the benefits.

The premise of acupuncture is to unblock the meridians or channels in the body through which chi moves.

Chi ('Ki' to the Japanese, 'Prana' to the Indians) is the inner-strength and intrinsic energy. No one English word could accurately define it. Nothing organic has existed without chi. Chi is responsible for all activity of the body, whether voluntary or involuntary. Furthermore, it generates power, it heals and it protects the body.

Chi, along with Jing and Shen, form a trinity of treasures for our well-being:

Jing: This genetic life force (or essence) is not cultivated. It is inherited from our parents. It determines the initial strength our constitutions and is responsible for growth in our bodies from conception to old age and all phases in between.

Shen: Chinese philosophies differentiate between different aspects of the spirit. Shen is that spirit responsible for mental awareness. It works within the mind to develop the personality.

Blood and other body fluids: are also considered vital substances regarding moistening and nourishing the body.

Chi: Of all the vital substances, chi is undoubtedly the most celebrated. Proper flow of this energy regains and sustains health, rejuvenates, it slows the aging process and it helps you find the fullest capabilities of your body. But this is only the beginning of the powers chi is reputed to possess.

Supernormal abilities have been attributed to the cultivation of chi: imperviousness to injury, uncanny strength or power, the ability to alter one's own mass, levitation, projecting unseen force without direct contact, etc. Many of these can be chalked up to parlour tricks. Perhaps, you've seen spears snap as they are pushed into a "master." Usually, the snap is created by the hands of the pusher not the presenter.

The breaking of concrete blocks can be impressive. Often the blocks are dosed in lighter fluid and set on fire to add an element of danger. The reality is the fire heats the blocks, thus weakening the cohesive bonds.

Something else to try when you get a moment; soak a phone book in water, then dry it slowly in the oven, pressed between to pans to keep it flat. Once it is dry, you can impress your friends with your superhero quality, as you tear the phonebook in half.

Maybe you're disappointed... you wanted those powers to be obtainable. Admit it, you wanted to believe you can develop your spirit to the level where such phenomenon are possible. Well, maybe you can.

> *All men secretly believe they are capable of being superheroes... it's true... growing up reading Superman, Batman, Spider-man... these aren't fantasies, these are options!*
> - Jerry Seinfeld

When chi, which remains internal, affects the outside of the body or the aura, which surrounds it most closely, we call this external kung. The body may become impervious to injury to varying degrees depending on the proficiency of the cultivator. A practitioner may develop bag kung to protect his abdomen, iron broom kung to protect his shins, forearm kung or head kung to protect their namesakes. Even groin kung can be developed. In demonstrations, Sifu and I often demonstrates this "splitting the peaches" kung technique. As he delivers, otherwise hospitalizing kicks between my legs, audiences are bewildered. I have sound positioning and the ability to remove my mind from the region, thus eliminating pain. But this is not the truest level of groin kung, as I am still vulnerable to front thrust kicks. The truest level can only be attained if the practitioner begins prior to puberty, during the time when the testicles descend, as it requires leaving that cavity open as a portal.

At the highest level of external kung, the aura becomes a tangible force field protecting the entire body, even from blades. Can this protect from bullets? If you could travel back 100 years and ask the rebel warriors of the Boxer rebellion, they wouldn't be able to answer. They were already dead from bullet wounds inflicted 101 years ago. They learned the hard way, everything has a limit.

Chi cultivation can lead to abilities where strength and power are increased. Iron palm and Iron fist are examples of this. With them, a person can use the fore mentioned parts of the hand to smash solid rock. Note, I'm not referring to boards or bricks, but actual stone produced by the earth. Some cultivators can manipulate air or the energies therein, to create channels of wind. A humble example of this is snuffing a candle from as many as ten metres away.

To be immovable as a rhino, or light as a squirrel able to run on treetops, are techniques of chi development.

Levitation and invisiblity? Well, I let you decide for yourself.

Despite the unbelievablity of these feats, no one educated in chi cultivation claims they are magic. It is considered an advanced science.

Consider the affects of adrenaline. When the medulla portion of the brain senses fear or other equally powerful emotions, it sends a signal to the adrenal glands, which are positioned above the kidneys. The glands release adrenaline into the system. Adrenaline allows us to perform outside our normal range of physical adeptness.

I believe through chi cultivation one can create a state of consciousness which is not fear, but, nevertheless, informs the medulla to trigger, the adrenal glands; thus, causing the same hypernormal abilities to manifest. Other attributes for which chi is reportedly responsible are not explainable through science –That is to say, not yet.

Yin, Yang and the Universe

Scientists have not yet solved all of the world's mysteries. However, it would be wrong not to acknowledge the vast number of answers they have brought to light.

Most of us tend to think that gravity and electro-magnetism are rudimentary concepts to scientists, but there are still questions regarding these forces. Still, scientists know enough to create magic of their own. For example, using the power of electro-magnetism they can cause an object to levitate.

Suppose that there are energies within our bodies that scientist know less about than they do gravity and electro-magnetism. Now, suppose there are people in this world with such supreme control over these energies they can use them to oppose gravity or bend light.

There are two widely accepted theories regarding all existence:
1) The general theory of relativity, which affirms the concept of an expanding universe, where the curvature of space and time are affected by all events.
2) Quantum mechanics, which are properties regarding things smaller than a molecule. Unlike the general theory of relativity, this branch of reasoning seems to preclude gravity.

The great mission for today's scientist is to unify these two theories.

Scientific procedure involves breaking down things into their smallest components. For a long time, we believed the tiniest of these building blocks were electrons, protons and neutrons, which compose atoms. Since then, quarks have been discovered. Thus far, there appear to be a half a dozen different types of quarks.

Energies have been categorized into only four different forces: gravity, electro-magnetism, weak nuclear force and strong nuclear force. It has been speculated that these forces are in fact, just one force that appears different under different circumstances. Since both external and intrinsic energies are a part of nature, this hypothesis can be extended to include them both.

My suspicion is that quarks, too, are all the same; varying in their appearance because of their circumstances.

Eventually, scientists will discover that everything in the universe is made up of only two components: the "this" and the "that" (Of course, knowing scientists, these components will likely be dubbed the "this" and the "anti-this"). Perhaps, one will appear as matter and the other as energy, perhaps not. These components will be without contention, flowing into each other; opposites necessary for each other's existence - Opposites as a harmonious fact of nature.

More Than A Little Homesick

I moved out of my parent's home when I was 18. I returned to the nest twice over the next 13 years. One summer, I needed to save money for a trip to Europe, and years later, after I returned from Japan, I had no place to live. However, I would guess, since I first moved out, I have spent at least one day at home per week.

It's a good feeling to have a haven to return to when life gets stressful. If you had a sheltered "Brady Bunch" childhood, as I did, what could feel safer than your parents' house? The moment I walked in the door, relaxation and security settled on me like a warm fog.

My parents moved out of that house this week. When I return home to visit, it will be in a house I've never seen.

I'm happy for them though. In particular, this will be good for my mother. A year and a half ago, my grandmother died. She lived in that house for almost two decades. She was the jewel of our family. And she was one of my best friends. Ma and I both gave eulogies at Granny's funeral. The last words Ma said were, "She was my pal."

For the last 18 months my mother would step out of her bedroom everyday and expect to see her pal sitting in her chair in her parlour at the end of the hall. It was too much.

Thinking of them sorting through all our things in order to pack properly, made me miss home a wee bit. Missing Stacey's wedding drove the blade of homesickness in deep.

Stacey is Brad's little sister; this makes her mine and Kevin's little sister, as well. I've known her almost my entire life. We've got a lot of history. Stacey's favourite story happened when I was eleven.

Brad was away at hockey camp, while I was still home in the neighbourhood (sending me to hockey camp would've been like sending a penguin to flight school). Stacey turned to me when some young, roustabout decide to rough her up. I found him and explained the code of chivalry to him with a sound thrashing. Later that day, I discovered that Stacey had actually accosted the boy. She challenged him to a scrap, and after he had gotten the better of her, she ran to me. She must still have a bit of the devil in her, because she still laughs when she tells the tale.

Some of my closest friends were there for the biggest day of her life, so far. But I was not. To make things more difficult, I received a painful email about the event from Kevin. He and Janice broke up two weeks ago. Both were at the wedding. He described how hard it was seeing her there without being able to be close to her. He couldn't kiss her, he couldn't hold her hand, he couldn't be the one responsible for her laughter, and it caused him to ache inside.

He's feeling those emotions I felt less than a year ago. I feel like a terrible friend for not being there.

Friendship is the most valuable thing on this earth. It pains me to be useless to my friends. Rich's separation occurred just before I left for Taiwan. It was the one factor that almost kept me from leaving. Hours of inner debate finally convinced me that Rich would be fine, even if I didn't move in with him. I suppose Kev will be fine, too, but he deserves my support.

To summarize, it would have been a good week to be home.

Culture Shock

Homesickness is not the same as culture shock. In fact, it's not necessarily even a symptom. I must confess, though, I may be experiencing a little of it.

That would explain why I was so miserable to Mei-shen yesterday morning. She contributed to my being late for a meeting and I acted like she deliberately disrespected me. I've since apologized for over-reacting. That kind of emotional over-reacting is a symptom.

I'm happy to say it's a minor symptom. Culture shock can result in severe cynicism, being judgmental and minor paranoia, as it did for me in Japan. That's not the case here. Some of my colleagues, who arrived in Taiwan from various western countries, at the same time I did, experienced it stronger than me. Between the first three weeks and the first two months, they already packed it in and headed for their homelands.

Still, I'd have to say that for Westerners, Taiwan is an easier adjustment than Japan. In Japan, I saw some of my coworkers crack.

If you have a disorder of any kind, culture shock will remove your ability to hide it. I saw a pathological liar lose touch with reality. I saw an alcoholic plummet into his illness. I even witnessed a nervous breakdown. These people had problems before, but when the shock crept up on them, their inner-demons became visible monsters. It's true what you've been told; you can't run away from your problems.

More Family

My junior brother, Mike has arrived from Canada. He, too, has a profound interest in Chinese culture. He fancies himself both a playboy and a Buddhist... Yes, these seem contradictory to me, as well. But, Mike is young and as such can convince himself of anything.

My understanding is that Buddhists strive to rid themselves of such distractions as greed, vanity and lust. Mike's youthful folly amuses me; not only does he not strive to rid himself of these traits, he revels in them. This makes him a lot of fun to hang out with.

Personally, I've tried to eliminate those weaknesses from my life. Greed has not been an issue. I've never felt it. I've known shameful vanity, but I've surprised myself at how easily I've diminished it. It's been so long since I've looked in a mirror I've almost forgotten what I look like.

Lust has been a difficult opponent.

Macho Crap?

The following article, is one from a regular column entitled <u>Betel Nut Buzz</u>, in the entertainment section of <u>The China Post</u> (printed and circulated in Taiwan, R.O.C. Friday, August 10, 2001):

Betel Nut Buzz
  by J. Boyce

> *The 'they are just like the folks back home' syndrome is on e of the most persistent and widely held misconeptions of the Western world, if not the whole world... Simply talking about 'cultural differences' and how we must respect them is a hollow cliche*
> *-Edward Hall, 'Beyond Culture'*

THE START OF THE PERFECT DAY: You are nearly sideswiped by a scooter, get bumped three times on a subway, and punch in at the office a minute late. Chalk it up to fate. Or, if you are like many foreigners, attribute it with a grumble to inability of Taiwanese to drive properly, look where they are walking, or trust employees to show up at work on time. (And why do some people eat with their mouths open, anyway?)

There are those who claim, "Deep down, people are the same everywhere." But unless they mean we all have bones, blood, brains and bums, or that we are all capable of hate and love, experience shows otherwise. There's a reason we have the term "culture shock" - It's because people are not the same. Different places have different rules and this includes everything from what constitutes personal space on the subway to how people treat the elderly, from what are considered appropriate eating manners to barroom brawl etiquette.

Take five Chinese guys beating up an American outside a Taipei club on a Saturday night. "Cowardly" is the response of most Westerners toward the Chinese. These Westerners believe in a "fair fight," which is at worst a one-on-one battle and at best a struggle where the two combatants possess roughly equal skills (images of a 19th-century gun duel come to mind).

But from a Taiwanese perspective, it makes no sense to give someone who has already angered you the chance to also defeat you in physical battle. Why risk injury when, with a little help from friends, you can be assured of victory? ...

How many Westerners could ever get used to this "five-on-one" style, no matter how long they lived here or how much they understood the culture? Not many, I would guess, because "deep down" it doesn't feel right to them..."

The following letter was my response, which they never printed:

Dear Betel-Nut Buzzer,

Last week you printed an article denouncing the myth that deep down people all over the world are the same. As an experienced traveler, I concur. The cultures in which we grow up mold members of their societies differently.

One of the examples you gave compared the Taiwanese perspective of physical conflict with the North American perspective. You stated that the Taiwanese wouldn't be as hesitant to outnumber their opponents; an act most North Americans would consider cowardly.

Coincidently, only one day after reading your article, I was witness to such an occurrence. Outside a nightclub, Saturday night I saw several men engaged in some hostility. I considered it none of my business and chose not to get involved.

I watched as a young Chinese woman sought to diffuse the situation. The hostility escalated and I continued to keep my distance.

Then it happened, a punch was thrown. Shockingly, the young woman was hit. One of the men hit her so hard she dropped to the ground and was immobile. I rushed to her to check on her condition and keep her from additional injury.

When I looked up I realized this conflict was not between two groups. Rather it was one man pitted against ten others. I consider this to be the second most cowardly act of the night (the first being, hitting an innocent woman). The lone man called out for my help. Hoping to protect the woman from further abuse, I made the decision to enter the fracas.

My attempt to persuade them to desist was futile; they detested foreigners. In fact, it was the sight of an interracial couple that provoked them. In a moment, I found myself alone against ten enraged men. They seemed crazed. If not for years of Shaolin Kung fu training I would have been permanently injured or worse. As it was, I punished them.

You may think this experience would encourage me to agree with your perspective. However, despite the misfortune of this event, I would say your assessment of Taiwanese men is unfair.

I recall an incident in my hometown of Windsor, Canada many years ago. I was attacked by six Americans who'd come over from Detroit, Michigan with the sole purpose of stirring up trouble. One incident mirrors the other.

Would it be fair for me to presume all Americans are dishonourable and cowardly as a result of dealing with a mere fraction of their populace? Of course not. Likewise, it is not right for you to judge all Taiwanese based on whatever incident compelled you to write your article. On the surface, it sounds like it aspires to racial understanding, but it has an overtone of prejudice.

Our cultures differ. We are not the same. But all societies are composed of warriors and non-warriors. One needn't be a warrior to comprehend honour and to be honourable. Many (perhaps most) non-warriors are worthy of respect. But unfortunately, every society also possesses cowards, worthy only of shame.

Incidentally, you may wonder why I was left alone against the ten assailants. The man who asked for my help, disappeared the moment I created a diversion, abandoning me to the horde. He was a North American.

Sincerely,
(Name withheld by request)

Did I do the right thing? Those men were bent on bludgeoning this couple because they were interracial. And as mentioned in the letter, they were crazed. They weren't just trying to bruise me or my ego. They wanted to inflict permanent damage - **at least**. In a moment, the street was chaotic with fists and feet, knees and elbows, beer bottles and bicycles. One of them actually swung a ten-speed bike against my thorax. I handed out three concussions and some busted ribs before those that remained standing, with their mouths bleeding and/or blackened eyes, decided to quit.

Macho crap? A barbaric display of my only true talent? I'm risking that kind of ridicule by including this journal in my book. But, what might have happened to that young woman or that young man, if I hadn't intervened? I can't feel bad about my decision.

Late August, 2001

Mei-shen and I broke up.

September, 2001

I'm finally doing it; I'm starting on my Master's degree. Athabasca University in Alberta, Canada has a well-respected, long distance education curriculum. I have been accepted into the Master's of Arts, Integrated Studies program.

As 'integrated' would imply, the program takes a holistic approach to studying the humanities: literature, history, philosophy, theology, etc. I was hoping to find a program that combines the arts and humanities with science. I have very little background in science, but the idea of exploring spirituality through a scientific approach, has become a fascination for me recently. Nevertheless, this course sounds challenging enough for someone who hasn't been on the receiving end of formal academics in years.

The course is peer-motivated via computer conferencing. I confess I'm a little intimidated by the intellectuals I have been in contact with thus far.

3 months

Three months without a journal entry... shameful, I admit.

Pursuit of higher education has been demanding. My classmates and I expected a program designed for people leading lives, with full time jobs, would be more flexible with its time constraints. **We were wrong.**

About a third of the class dropped out within a month. Some wrote letters of complaint, pointing out that this one class had the workload of three and that it was supposed to be geared towards people who hadn't time to attend university. The professor, Dr. Derek Briton, had a very simple explanation; it is a Master's level course. I have to agree. It was challenging and time consuming... and I wouldn't have it any other way. It makes me feel worthy of the praise given to me by the professor and my peers who once intimidated me.

My final paper, <u>Sex and Spirituality</u>, was a bit removed from the avenues the professor was encouraging us to research. However, he was pleased. More importantly, I was pleased.

I wish I was as pleased with everything else I've pursued during these last three months. My training has been stagnant. I do everything I've always done, but without a class and without Sifu, it's not as inspiring. I have not yet been successful in finding anyone of my Kung Fu lineage teaching in Taiwan, Wu Heng Li or otherwise. I have a couple leads to follow, but that's all.

I have also been in and out of another relationship already. This young lady seemed so right in many ways. But, like so many others she broke my rule of having only one man in her life at a time. Is that such a difficult rule? It turned out, not only had she lied to me about breaking up with her previous boyfriend, they were still living together. He and I found out about each other on Christmas day... not the best Christmas I've ever had!

Some of you might be thinking, "Oh hell, no! Is he going back to that bitter, Robert-Plantesque "soul-of a-woman-was-created-below" style of writing?"

Relax, I'm fine. Surprisingly, I only hated her for a day. I feel bad for her, really. Her problem isn't her heart, it's her head. And I hope she gets it straight someday. Then she can stop setting herself up for punishment and start allowing herself to be happy.

Why am I handling this without so much bitterness? Ya' got me. Maybe it's a result of my relationship with Mei-shen. Though things didn't work out between us, I know she's a wonderful person. I know she had a healing affect on me.

Chinese New Year

Chinese New Year was fantastic. Howard and I had been looking forward to this for some time, as we have been able to spend as much time together over the last year as we had hoped. Howard has guilt in his voice when we speak of it. He blames himself because he's a workaholic, but it's not entirely his fault. He lives right in the heart of Taipei and I live out in county without reliable transportation. This problem will soon be rectified. I'm moving into the city next month. We'll see lots more of each other.

Our trip started with Howard, Mike and I at Howard's grandparent's house in Gaoshung with Howard's family. From what I can see, there are three important elements to Chinese New Year: red decorations on the door, random outbursts of firecrackers, and platters upon platters of food. If you're a Westerner, imagine Thanksgiving for seven days.

The red banners and the firecrackers have the same purpose: to frighten away the New Year's monster. Trying to imagine a monster that fears the colour red and trembles over loud noises, makes me picture something akin to Grover from Sesame Street. However, before anyone of us occidentals make judgments we need to recall the original purpose of hanging mistletoe, or explain how dressing up as goblins on All Hallow's Eve will frighten away other goblins. Many traditions don't carry with them their original beliefs, but I believe they're important, nonetheless. They maintain a culture.

On one morning of our trip, Howard's mom invited me for an outing. (I've taken to calling her Auntie. I never felt right calling her Julie, but 'Ms. Chang' is just too formal considering the evolution of our relationship.) She informed me on this trip that she considers me part of the family. Though she knows little of Kung Fu, she recognizes me as Howard's big brother.

Auntie, Howard, his uncle and I hiked up Sho Mountain that morning; a venture as pleasing for the eyes as it is healthy for the body. It was very scenic and tea-time was very relaxing, but what I enjoyed most was our lunch with a clan of monkeys. They didn't fear us at all. They sit as close to you as do dear friends. Of course, it's still a bad idea to touch them. A bite from a monkey can be terribly infectious. Only one other animal carries more potential to spread a disease... so try not to get bitten by any humans either. I didn't actually suspect that I would get bitten, but I didn't take the chance. I wasn't concerned that I wouldn't get to a hospital in time to get the necessary shots should one prove infectious. I just didn't want to be the guy on the six o'clock news who was too stupid not to touch the monkey.

Mike had already returned to Taipei when Howard and I decided to spend a night with his father in Taichung. You wouldn't notice this home amidst the park of warehouses. From the outside it looks just like one of them. Inside is a large home where we invited for more food and drink by Howard's dad's business partners. As I sat with Howard, his dad and our "uncles", they began to pour rice wine into us.

I learned that it is customary to show your appreciation of someone's company by a seated toast, humble enough not to disrupt the conversation, after which you both down the remainder of your glass. On this sort of occasion, to drink without offering this minor salutation to someone, or to reject is considered rude.

As I was a newcomer, considered to be Howard's older brother, and as Howard's company was considered a rare treat, most toasts fell upon us. Howard and I were beginning to stagger very early in the evening, but it seemed we couldn't distract them from poisoning us further. Howard quipped, "I'm so glad you're finally here to experience my culture, Jay... no one has understood my pain." I don't recommend laughing while drinking rice wine; it really stung my nostrils.

February 14th fell in the middle if this year's vacation. One year to the day I arrived in Taipei. New Years is a time to look both into the past and into the future. I took a moment to consider what I had accomplished since a year ago. I came up with nothing. I'm not financially stronger. I have no romantic partner. I haven't found Sigung Wu. I don't even speak Chinese yet.

In rereading the preceding words I realize I am not being fair with myself.
*I have started earning my Master's degree.
*I have acquired survival knowledge of Mandarin Chinese (so far).
*I haven't succumbed to culture shock or homesickness.
*I have again been blessed by making new wonderful friends.
***I have healed in a multitude of ways.**

One needs to remind oneself of such things, or it's all fruitless.

Does abiding in the Tao mean that I shouldn't concern myself with such things?

March 31st, 2002

Five people were killed by the earthquake yesterday.

All five were killed right here in my neighbourhood by machinery and concrete which fell from a building currently under construction. This building is intended to be the tallest in the world. The Tower of Babel is to be erected in a country known for its powerful earthquakes.

Arrogance!

Early April, 2002

I frequent Sun Yat Sen Memorial Park these days. Many Kung Fu practitioners use its grassy parks or concrete patios for training, as do Chi Kung practitioners, dancers, cheerleaders, in-line skaters and kite flyers.

I've been following up some leads regarding Seven Star Praying Mantis instructors. A kind gentleman named Sifu Adam Chu, who no longer teaches Mantis directs me to another man I hadn't heard of before.

I soon remember what I discovered in Japan regarding the martial arts; North America does not have a monopoly on arrogance and ignorance. I inform this other teacher, whom I prefer to leave nameless, that I am searching for someone whose lineage is connected to mine. He answers this question by asking me to show him the first two movements of Bung Bu. I do. Then with a superfluous air of confidence he informs me that mine is the Hong Kong lineage.

Wrong.

To begin, I didn't ask him my lineage. I know my lineage. It does not involve Hong Kong. The first thing he should have done was listen to the question.

Despite this, I go to him a second time to acquire about any leads he may have unturned. I was unaware that he wasn't going to bother doing any checking, since he presumed that I would naturally want to train under him. Over the course of a very long 40 minutes of this second meeting, he mentioned three times that he began training when he was six years old. I mentioned that I began learning math when I was four years old, but that I still couldn't balance my cheque book. Worse than that I heard comments on the poor quality of North American schools of Kung Fu. He'd been to **one** once. Worst of all he told me that my Sifu probably didn't teach Chin Na properly. (Chin Na are joint locking, joint manipulation and pressure point techniques.) My Sifu's teachings are those that enabled me to remove ex-convict murders and drug users from a flophouse where I worked several years ago. My Sifu's teachings are those that have earned my friend, Rich the respect of the City of Windsor's Hospitals Administration and the Windsor Municipal Police Dept. and for his ability to restrain psychotics during his time as an orderly in the psycho ward.

I was livid. I am embarrassed to say I almost considered challenging him or any of his top students to engage me. I was able to excuse myself without succumbing to my ego. No sense in reducing myself to barbarism and soiling the name of our school, just to prove a point to this twit.

The West certainly has no monopoly on arrogance and ignorance, and the East has no monopoly on knowledge and expertise.

The same can be said of youth and age. Not only the young are ignorant. Announcing that you "started learning 50 years ago" doesn't tell me as much about you, as answering the question, "When did you stop?"

Tony

As I said, most of my experiences with other teachers have been positive. Several months ago, after participating in an instructor's demonstration at the National Taiwan University, I was approached by Tony Clark. Tony is also an instructor of Seven Star Mantis and was intrigued by the similarities and differences of our lineages.

Tony's lineage descends from Lo Gwan Yu. He was famous as a renovator of the art. Lo Gwan Yu taught Chun Chun Yee, who taught Gregory Fong. Tony is Sifu Fong's disciple. To continue with the family terminology, as I prefer, Tony is my Sifu's cousin.

I realize this gets kind of messy. Perhaps this chart can make it clear:

```
                      She Shao Dao Ren
                   (within the Shaolin Temple)
                              |
                         Li San Chen
                              |
                       Wong Rong Shang
                              |
                         Fan Yu Tang
                              |
            ----------------------------
            |                           |
      Lin Ching Shan              Lo Gwan Yu
            |                           |
    Wang Tsung Ching            Chun Chun Yee
            |                           |
       Wu Heng Li                Gregory Fong
            |                           |
   Simon Pszczonak               Tony Clark
            |
        Jay McCoy
```

I mention this now because Tony has been gracious enough to offer to teach Mike and me. If it seems ironic to you that I'm being taught by an Occidental North American in Taiwan, then you're missing the big picture. I have been searching for someone whose lineage is closely connected to my own. Four generations is as close as I've come. And Tony's forms are the most similar to ours of any Mantis school I've ever encountered.

I am additionally fortunate, because Tony has, thus far, been a great instructor. Small wonder; the man has not only been a practitioner for many years, but an avid researcher. He's as knowledgeable in the history of our art, as anyone I've met, including my own Sifu. By the time this book comes out Tony will have completed his Ph.D. in Chinese Literature. The study of literature, of course, includes researching history and culture. His fluency and access to resources has supplied Tony with a wealth of knowledge. His memory seldom fails him when he's relaying his studies. He's brilliant, to say the least.

Sadly, Tony returns to Portland, Oregon in a month to write his dissertation. So, my tutelage under him will be short-lived. Selfish bastard; moving on with his own dreams with no concern for me.

Mid-May, 2002

"All my words come back to me,
in shades of mediocrity,
like emptiness and harmony..."
          -Paul Simon

As I reread my most recent journals I notice two things: 1) That I am writing less frequently than I was before. 2) My entries are becoming more and more emotionally stifled. This leads me to consider the possibility that I'm running out of things to say.

My closest friends will be shocked by this. "Jay with nothing to say? Not our Jay... Mr. I've-got-an-opinion-and-you're-gonna'-hear-it." But I suppose it was inevitable that after 15 months of writing, I would reach a lull. After all, this is my life, not some fictitious piece of work, were you should expect some climactic conclusion. At least not without me dying; and I'm not prepared to make that sacrifice for my literary goals.

So, I question; do I end my book here, with a whisper? Perhaps, if you've developed a connection to me through my writings you'll find comfort in knowing that I've recovered from distrust and bitterness, that I'm confident I will always find solace abiding in the Tao, and that I will continue to strive for personal betterment.

Yawn! Is that a whisper or a whimper? Surely, there must be a grander moment yet to come which I can offer as my adieu.

Have patience, my reader, and I'll try not to let you down.

Sabrina

Why haven't I written about Sabrina earlier? It's as though I'm not taking it seriously, unless I put her name to paper. But we've been dating exclusively for two months. My third attempt at a relationship in a year and half... does that make me desperate or in high-demand? Let's go with the more flattering depiction.

I've been trying to act like it's not significant. Perhaps, it hasn't been; but, tonight, I lie here and think about her. I question what has caused my emotions to plateau.

I've been good to her, but not overly expressive about my feelings, only because I'm not certain what those feelings are.

She's been wonderful to me. I don't think any woman has treated me this good since high school.

That's it, isn't it? Because even those high school romances change. She's young enough to treat me with girlish adoration, but she may grow out of it.

Last night, I told her how I've seen women change and I issued a warning: "If I begin talking about a future together, about the seriousness of our relationship, about love, you'd better not change. Of course, people are going to grow; that's not what I mean. If you stop being this wonderful person, once you think you've got me, **I will walk away.**" I think the threat wasn't as significant to her, as the fact that I acknowledged the potential for a future together.

Tonight, I find myself daydreaming about the possibility of her meeting my friends back home, of her experiencing a Canadian Christmas, and other possibilities. So, progress is being made. I still miss Mei-shen, but, the truth be told, even after 7 years, I still miss Mutsumi. After Mu-chan and I broke up, I didn't enter into another romance for three years. I still compare other women to her. That's a lot for anyone to live up too. Maybe Sabrina is capable, maybe she's not. I owe it to myself to find out.

Hong Kong

My recent trip to Hong Kong was very close to terrible. Even before I left Taipei, the problems began; I was heavily fined for over-staying my visa. That meant I went to Hong Kong with considerably less money than I had planned.

With limited funds, I chose to stay in the ghetto of Kowloon. On my previous trip, I never made it to Kowloon, so this was a plus for me.

Things only turned sour after dinner. I'd had a delicious Szechwan dish of beef and noodles. I, of course, asked the contents before hand. The manageress neglected to mention any shellfish. But as I was in the hospital struggling to breathe an hour later, obviously my allergy had been triggered.

I spent two hours there, before they released me. The antihistamines swimming inside me, wiped me out. So, even with my room in the slum, with loud neighbours arguing in languages neither English nor Chinese, sleep came easy. That is until two a.m. The police raided my hostel, pounding on all the doors and insisting on seeing our passports. I was in Hong Kong legally; I got to stay. Many of my neighbours weren't so lucky.

On Monday, after taking care of business at the Taiwan consulate, I moved myself to the Causeway Bay area where I have stayed on previous trips. The price had gone up since three months ago, but it was considerably nicer. Still, it being a Monday night and me having little cash, it was quite dull.

The saving grace of my trip came Tuesday. I picked up my visa and had several hours to spare before my flight. I spent them in the Hong Kong Park. I sat still for long periods of time just admiring the beauties of the park: the waterfall, the fountain, the trees, the birds... mostly the birds.

The park has an aviary containing species that seem quite alien to me. There is the great pied hornbill, so large and colourful, a proud example of nature's artistry. A Rothchild's myrah bird swooped down by my brow and landed only two yards away. He can't hide among the green as his plumage is as white as fine ivory. Hull myrahs gather to gossip. Black and white with orange bills, and chubby enough to deceive you into believing penguins had finally learned to fly. A pelican graces the exit. In photos and on television, this species appears comical, maybe even ridiculous. But up close and in person, he is majestic in appearance and mannerism. Blue-tailed fairy blue birds, crowned partridges, yellow budgies accessorize the foliage, bright and shiny like moistened Popsicles.

Eventually, I pull myself away from the aviary, to explore the rest of the park. I walk up the hill to a courtyard. "Tai Chi Court" the sign reads, but no one is there practicing. After a few minutes of exploration, the spirit moves me. I am stepping, stomping, and soaring through the movements of the Seven Star forms. I am awarded the rare satisfaction of dancing through all my forms without an error. Content, I plant myself once again in a more public area and enjoy doing nothing for a while.

Testing Sabrina

I look for problems and find none. It's almost frustrating... no one can be this good... what's left for me to do but accept it... this might just work out.

A few weeks ago, about the time I first mentioned her in my journals, I called her out, so to speak. "If we're still together when I choose to return to Canada, will you be going with me?" I'm not demanding that we ship off to Canada this year, or even next year, or for that matter, the year after. I was basically demanding proof of her level of commitment... not that she's aware that was my intention.

The ball is in her court.

Is that where I want the ball?

Gao Dao Shung

I'd been hearing good things about the old man. Finally, Howard and I managed to locate him. He's teaching in a basement in a part of town very far from my home.

Their seven-star lineage separates from ours as far back as the 2nd generation from the temple. Nevertheless, their forms are even more similar to ours, than those of Tony's school. Obviously, this is because their teachings, too, haven't been blessed/cursed with the renovations of Lo Gwan Yu.

He's a kindly gentleman, who welcomed us warmly. He demonstrates very little, but still seems rather lively; more like a man in his mid-60s than his late 80s.

All of his 20 or so students showed promise, and at least two moved marvelously. They reminded me of my brothers, Dave Chaborek and Craig Durocher, two of the finest form stylists in our school. Most importantly, I liked the atmosphere of the school. They're a family like ours, I think.

For me, it was fun and educational. Howard may join the school. Howard has no intention of returning to Canada to live, so this school might be just what he needs to rekindle his passion. Howard was sensational. Now, he's digressed to just very good. A school and schedule could repair that.

Unfortunately, although Sifu Gao was aware that descendents of Ling Ching Shan had migrated to Taiwan, he knows nothing of the whereabouts of my Sigung nor anyone connected with him.

My Job

The most observant readers have noticed that I have avoided talking about my job. Perhaps you've also deduced that I am a teacher. This is the job I was fired from almost two years ago.

Despite the suspiciousness of my dismissal, it had left me doubtful. Although the voice that has been telling me that I'm not a good teacher has been growing gradually quieter over the last year and half, I have avoided talking about my job until now. Finally, I believe that voice has been silenced. I accepted my promotion today. I am head teacher of Jeh-Mah-Jie English Immersion School.

Some of the mothers have told our owner/operator that I am the best teacher they've ever seen. This has been supported by letters I've received from some of them. As far as I know, every one of my colleagues and the parents are pleased with the decision to promote me, because, **I am a good teacher.**

I took a couple of days to consider the promotion. It will involve more hours that I don't want to sacrifice. This will mean I must delay my next course towards my Master's until January. Of course, my bigger concern is training time.

I have decided to allow myself one month in which to slack off in my training. Not to say, I won't train, but that I will reduce my hours significantly for the month of August. This should be enough time to adjust to my new duties.

*   *   *

The question is no longer am I capable of being a primary school teacher, but do I want to be one. As much as I love those kids, and am thrilled to see them progressing, I'm not content. Presenting "See spot run. Run, Spot, run," in manners that are stimulating to the children takes some creativity; but it's still "See Spot run."

High school may be more intriguing, but even more so I'd like to teach at a college or university. That's partly why I am working towards my Master's degree. But studying has to be a part-time responsibility, when working is a full-time one.

I've been teaching adults for years in Shaolin Kung Fu and it is greatly rewarding. It is, however, only for the emotional rewards. I am grimly aware, that it's unfeasible to try and earn a living at it. In a metropolitan city, with a huge market, it is difficult. In Essex County, which I call home, it's virtually impossible.

Some More Sabrina

She took weeks to consider, which was right to do. This is a major life change we're talking about, not something to be taken lightly. One year ago, Mei-shen answered "no"; and you know how that turned out.

Sabrina returned a verdict of "yes". And something has come alive in me. I'm not sure what they are; I believe some people call them "feelings".

I wasn't aware of how much I'd hardened my heart until she gave me her answer. I must have been holding back, because in that moment it was like the rock was smashed and a river of devotion flowed through me.

It feels good... and it may not last... she may let me down yet... but right now, it feels good.

The Search Continues (in Taichung)

Frustrated by the fruitlessness of my quest for Sigung Wu, I ventured back to Taichung this weekend. If not for the fact that Sabrina and I had a lot of fun getting away together, the trip would have been a total waste. For two days, I met with as many Kung Fu and Tai Chi practitioners as I could. No one knows of him. If he is, in fact, living in the Taichung area, he trains in solitude. Much as I suspected, he doesn't bother with organizations. I suppose he has little use for them, he once told Sifu to be leery of them.

Internet, telephone directories, organizations, and word of mouth, have all turned up nothing. I'm afraid I may have to give up the search.

Mid-October

As I promised myself, I've held to a strict training regimen since September. All aspects have been focused on: forms, applications, stance training, iron palm, speed training, plyometrics, power training, acrobatics, endurance training, chi kung, meditation, and historical research.

It doesn't require so much shirking of other responsibilities, but rather turning off the T.V.

I'm Dreaming of a White Christmas

It's been decided, Sabrina and I are going to spend Christmas in Canada. I'm sure it won't be a moment to soon. Lately, I've been homesick again.

Dreams of being with my friends and family make for restless sleep. Besides, I've been grumpy lately. I mean a real crab-ass. Sabrina deserves better than to have to listen to me gripe all the time. She says, she hasn't noticed me being irritable (bless her heart), but I feel it.

So, soon she'll be meeting all the people who are the core of my being. She's very excited about it... we both are.

Shugyo

"… it is necessary to purposely seek out new challenges which once were a part of the daily life of the warrior."

Dr. Alan Hasegawa

If there is an English or Chinese word for it, I don't know it. The Japanese call it Shugyo'. It is a severe training ritual. The purpose of which is to make clear your optimum capabilities. But, more so, its purpose is to call your spirit to surface. Major Forrest E. Morgan has described it thusly:

How many (people) know the limits of their physical and emotional capabilities? Do you? Do you know how fast you can run a mile, or how many miles you can run before you have to stop? Do you know how much weight you can lift or how many minutes you can fight against multiple opponents before you can't fight any longer? Do you know if you can climb, rappel, or even stand at the edge of of a sheer cliff without freezing in panic?

The warrior who applies shugyo in his training knows the things if they are related to his personal goals. Furthermore, if he senses weakness in these or other areas, he may add them to his goals or log them away for future challenges.

Morgan then discusses the timing and placing of such a ritual. It needn't be held in the training hall; in fact, that would prove limiting. It is not expected to be routine. It is most often an annual ritual. I hold mine once every 2 years. The time came last Sunday.

Morgan's first experience with shugyo came during a TaeKwonDo Training camp when he was 19. It reads only slightly more rigorous than one of our tougher classes at the Wu Shen Temple. I require more.

I can think of no fears left to face. I have rafted the white waters of the Ottawa River. I've climbed a mountain and been nearly squashed by a renegade boulder. I've been face to face with numerous wild animals. I've consumed the meat, blood and venom of a cobra. I've even jumped from an airplane. None of these brought fear or panic.

I suppose it may have to do with being born a severe asthmatic. I faced death many times as a sickly child. Bouts of pneumonia and bronchitis plagued my infant years. And nights as a boy, when I couldn't control my own lungs, I felt my bed was becoming my coffin. What scares a man after that?

At this time, I should mention about a year and a half ago, a cockroach crawled across my arm and I screamed like a 5-year-old girl.

Of course, it is impossible to test all of your capabilities in one day. You certainly can't sprint 100 metres and then accurately determine how far you can run before you drop. Nor could you hold your horse stance for your longest duration after pushing your maximum leg press.

The idea isn't necessarily to find all those individual limits. It's finding the drive to go on when you're pushed yourself beyond all sense.

"Winning…. Is when your body says its time to quit and your heart says, 'do it anyway.'"

Spider-man (as dictated by Gerry Conway in
Spectacular Spider-man #145)

I began early with my Falun Dafa (chi cultivation) exercises. Then to the gym where I tested my maximum bench press: the most I've ever done. The amount is laughable to most bodybuilders. But as a 167lb., 33 year old ectomorph, I'm proud of it. I continued with an arm workout, punishing my biceps and triceps.

Next I was off to the track, where I've been spending more time than usual the last 6 weeks. I ran as fast as I could, setting a personal best for 1 kilometre. Again, your average varsity track athlete wouldn't be impressed, but again, your average track athlete isn't a 33 year old, ectomorphic, asthmatic.

I didn't stop after 1 km. I continued to run for a total of 5 km. Following this, I spent 30 minutes stretching - the only logical choice.

A small lunch and 30 minutes rest spent meditating and I was back at it. Skipping and plyometrics filled the next half hour and 200 pushups filled the next 3 minutes. I stretched again before embarking on every form I know, twice. Here was a physical and mental challenge. Remembering the steps to every form and to execute them with grace and precision, while my body yearned for peace, was challenging enough. To add to that, all the while, Sabrina threw questions at me ranging from basic math to deep philosophy.

At last, it was time for the horse stance. My thighs screamed and my calves tightened and eventually I succumbed to gravity.

A full day's work completed! And how did I fill the evening? I got drunk with friends. After all, it was my birthday.

Christmas

It's not the same old house that I left behind nearly 2 years ago, But it's the same old couch I sit on and begin my reflection of the last couple of days. I've the Christmas tree to the right of me and to the left I've a view of my parent's backyard. The patio, lawn, fence and beyond have been painted Christmas white. It came just last night, Christmas Eve. It's as though I called it in and had it ordered at the perfect time to paint the perfect scene.

Watching the wind whip curls of it all about the yard brings an odd thought, 'Canada is so much warmer than Taiwan.' Of course, Canada achieves temperatures well below zero, and Taiwan does not. Taiwan is a sub-tropical/tropical island, but when it does get chilly there's no escaping it.

My apartment hasn't central heating and there's no insulation in Taiwanese houses. I didn't notice last winter; perhaps it was warmer or my old apartment held the heat better than my rooftop loft. Here in my parent's house, I sit barefoot, with sweatpants and a T-shirt, and think how cold it looks *out there*. We have that luxury.

I shouldn't overlook the possibility that my warmth is an emotional side effect. I have spent the last 2 days with my family and oldest and dearest friends. All of them seem to have taken well to Sabrina, and she to them... especially the dog. Sabrina adores Clancy and hangs on her every chance she gets. Clancy laps up the affection as if she were starved for it. That's a joke. She's been the center of attention in our household since the day my father brought her home.

Sabrina hasn't rested much. My fault, I suppose, but I've been excited to see everyone and eager to expose her to Canadianna. I've been successful, so far. We arrived late the first night, but the 4 hour drive from Toronto gave me a good chance to catch up with my folks. It also gave them an uninterrupted opportunity to get to know Sabrina.

When we arrived home, we were given a tour of the new place and the settled in for a ten hour sleep. We spent the morning with my mom, and in the afternoon the boys arrived. Kev, Brad, Rich and I took shots at each other over a few beers; much to the amusement of Sabrina and Ma.

The plan for the evening was proposed to me. I could join them on the ice tonight for a game of old-timer's pickup hockey. Between the four of us, we scrambled together enough equipment for me to play.

Among the other hack players was Sifu, so, our reunion was far from the formal confines of the school. Sabrina sat in the stands with Bridget, Rich's new live-in girlfriend (he appears to have recovered). Here Sabrina had her first taste of Canadian culture. Clumsy men on skates try to swat a puck between a goalie's legs.

Ours is the apology league. If two opposing players, so much as nudge each other, "Oh sorry!" can always be heard.

As a boy I was one of the worst players in my league. I stopped playing when I was 11. I didn't discover I had real athletic potential until puberty hit. Now, after years of honing my physical capabilities, I stride confidently across the rink, knowing that in this rag-tag assembly of hockey players, I have reached the esteemed level of average. (Sometimes, I even score.)

We crashed at Rich's that night and returned here in the morning. Ma took us grocery shopping. It was fun. No, I mean it. Only once before has Sabrina seen what North Americans would consider a real supermarket, and it wasn't as big as the one we were at yesterday.

Later, I took Sabrina with me to the cemetery to wish Granny a merry Christmas. We came home, wrapped presents and watched Christmas movies while discussing our holiday agenda with Ma and Pop. All in all, it was a pleasant Christmas Eve.

Today, she's experiencing her first Christmas. This includes Ma's traditional Christmas morning breakfast, meeting my brother and sister and their families, unwrapping the gifts she was surprised to receive, watching the kids have a frenzy, to finally just sitting back and relaxing… or as relaxed as she can be with my family bombarding her with questions. She often turns to me for reassurance. The wink and smile I send seems to be enough.

Soon, we'll gather for dinner. Ma. Pop, Uncle Gary, Scott, my sister-in-law, Cathy and their son, Nicky, Hayley, my brother-in-law, Ron, there kids Sara and Josh, Sabrina and I will all fit around that big dining room table and feast like royalty. Twelve tonight will join more tomorrow at my Auntie Norma's house.

We smile, we hug, we joke and laugh, and we'll look about the table and feel blessed to have each other. We'll miss Uncle Ernie. We'll miss Uncle Lyle. We'll miss Gramma and Grandpa. We'll miss Samantha, a baby girl from Scott and Cathy, whom we weren't given time to know. We'll miss my dog, Spencer. And, of course, we'll miss Granny, who left us most recently. But it's not too early to remember any of them with a smile rather than a tear.

That's part of Christmas, too, isn't it?

January 3rd, 2003

I said good-bye to all my buddies, before I got on this iron bird bound for Taipei. I suppose I should be filled with things to say, but the mind sometimes protects the heart, and I am left feeling numb… almost. I miss them already.

Feeling Bad

"I've never known a wild thing to feel sorry for itself. A frozen bird can fall dead from its bough without once having felt sorry for itself."
                                        D.H. Lawrence

"I can't complain, but sometimes I still do."
                                        Joe Walsh
                                        (as Keith Moon)

I shouldn't feel low. The voice inside my head is complaining about good things. I refer to it as "the voice in my head," because it couldn't really be me, could it? The intellectual scholar, stupid enough to focus on grey linings? The Taoist philosopher absorbed in self-pity?

I've a new place to live. My old place had a convenient location, but the small space started to press on me. Now, I have a place three times bigger, located at the foot hills of Yami Mountain. Not as convenient, but a pretty area, where real wilderness starts as soon as my street ends. The neighbourhood is home to pleasant people with helpful shops. Restaurants, produce stands, hardware stores, pharmacies, a video store, and, of course, two 7-11s. The stores are small inside, less than 3 big strides in any direction, but they recover from this size impairment by spilling out on to the sidewalks. Like any part of Taipei, the sidewalks are an obstacle course. It doesn't bother me though, because unlike most of Taipei, you can safely walk down the wide street unencumbered by cars.

The apartment is disgusting. That is to say, it's structurally sound and has potential, but it's the filthiest place I've stepped in since the sewage plants. It will require a lot of time and energy. This apartment is more money, too; money, I no longer have. As is standard policy in Taiwan, I had to give first and last month's rent and an equal amount for a deposit. I am choking financially. However, my new job pays better. I should be ahead of the game in a couple of months.

I've starting my new job at a beautiful new elementary school, way up on one of the mountains – The prestigious Kan-Chou Elementary (a.k.a Cambridge). This should be good news, but I'm a little deflated about the distance I must travel each day. I'm also feeling the pressure, which has already been thrown on me. I will be replacing a teacher, who was apparently a workaholic. His three classes were among the most advanced in the school. The school's English department is the cornerstone of its reputation. During my observations, this was pointed out to me roughly a bazillion times.

I don't sound very confident, do I?

Time and energy should rectify my problems. Except the big problem is I've no energy. I'm sick. Asthma trouble, I haven't suffered from asthma since I was thirteen, unless it was triggered by an allergic reaction. Apparently, something is amiss in the air these days. A week ago, Sabrina's friend had an asthma attack for the first time in several years. The doctor told her, she was one of many recent victims. He must have been an experienced doctor, in contrast to the young know-it-all I dealt with on my visit to the hospital.

Realizing that my bronchial spasms were getting worse, I arrived at the hospital around 10:30 p.m. I informed this novice doctor of my condition. After applying a stethoscope to my chest and listening to some melody in his head, rather my lungs, he said, "No, its not asthma." I raised an eyebrow, "it's not?"

"I don't hear any wheezing."

"You don't? I can hear it without a stethoscope. Sabrina?" She was two feet away. She defended my diagnosis, "I can hear it, too."

A grown man, who has had asthma his whole life, recognizes the problem. Believe me.

I instructed the doctor on how to treat it. After listening to my chest a second time, he concurred.

Within an hour, there was a woman my age, a man slightly older and an 8 year old boy in the room, all with the same problem. Rookie, M.D. was a little quicker to take them seriously.

I've since learned pneumonia has been spreading around Asia. Hong Kong, a common stop over for Taiwanese, has been seriously infected. Perhaps we acquired a milder strain of it here. I am ably to function for a short while, but I get fatigued easily. Being sick leaves you weak and vulnerable - Not how a warrior should feel. I haven't trained in a week.

It seems I have abandoned my Shaolin philosophies. There are people with real problems in the world, yet I seem unable to ignore my inner-voice whining over trivial shit.

I could manage sitting at the computer working on my university course, if I had a phone line. The phone company is tardy connecting my new phone. Which is also why I haven't been able to make contact with my family. I've been having disturbing dreams about them lately, so I'd like to check in.

All this negativity is like blasphemy to me. So much for riding the waves of life like a cork in the water. So much for the Taoist perspective of acceptance. So much for the way of nature. I'm disappointing myself and I don't know how to stop it.

How could D.H. Lawrence be sure that bird didn't feel sorry for itself?

From Bad To Worse

It was Friday night. I spent my first day at the new school and was observed teaching my grade 2 class. No problems arose. I was happy. Brian and I went bowling. It was a rough part of town called Ban Chiao, near my old apartment in Hsin Chuang, but we had old friends to visit out there before our celebration. I felt myself unwinding for the couple of hours we spent at the bowling alley.

We were stopped at a red light on our way home; sitting on Brian's motorcycle discussing unimportant things. Our chat was interrupted by a shouting man carrying a steel pipe. We looked at him confused for only a second and then **wham**, he hit Brian in the head with the pipe. We jumped off the bike and grabbed him. A moment later, we were surrounded by seven more with pipes, crowbars and a baseball bat. The ensuing frenzy continued even after the police arrived. All ten of us were sent to the hospital.

The police ordered the paramedics to give me a sedative, since I kicked a man in the face, even though they had already pulled me off him. He landed a crowbar over my left eye, tearing a gash now held together by six stitches. Brian was a bit luckier, suffering only a pair of black eyes.

Less lucky were the thugs who attacked us. The police informed us that five of them would have to remain in the hospital. Brian had broken one's leg and I broke another's arm. Brutal. Horrific. Even disgusting; but neccessary to save our lives. Of this, I'm certain.

The attackers' version of the story was ridiculous. Furthermore, bystanders backed-up what we told the police. They have no doubt about the truth, and have assured us the men will be prosecuted. But this is Taiwan. I won't hold my breath.

Lying in the hospital, after the sedatives wore off, I considered leaving Taiwan. This is twice, in as many years, that I've had to defend myself simply because I'm Caucasian. Why should I stay somewhere where I can't go out and have fun without looking over my shoulder for danger. I considered this a while. It pained me. Usually, I like Taiwan. I have no trouble finding work in my field. I've built up my references of people who genuinely respect my teaching ability. My life is often a beautiful exotic adventure, and only rarely an ugly exotic adventure, like Friday night. And I have Sabrina. She's not ready to leave. And I'm not ready to leave her. I could leave, just as Rosa Parks could have got her stubborn ass out of that bus seat. God bless her…

I'll stay.

I'll struggle to communicate everyday. The phone company will aggravate me like no company ever has. And now I'll start my job looking like a thug. But I'll stay.

Even Worse

With my phone finally connected, I called home give my folks my new number. My Uncle Gary is dead.

Uncle Gary was overweight and he drank a bit too much. I asked how it happened expecting it to be a related problem. My mother informed me that he had broken his ankle and died two days later.

It makes no sense to me, either.

Uncle Gary was apart of my every Christmas, every Easter and many summers by our pool or climbing his willow tree, when I was a boy. He always tried his best to make everyone in the room smile. He was a good man. I'm deeply saddened by his death.

Also, I feel more removed from my family than I ever have before. My cousins, Lauren, Monica, and Jeff gave eulogies for their father, which I didn't hear.

How far have I come in two years? My uncle's death is understandably depressing, but the other things are negligible. Maybe it is just time. Maybe the human condition is such that our minds can only function as happy for so long. Sadness, even without justification, is a part of the necessary balance; satisfying the yin/yang of our psychology.

Many self-help books suggest putting our troubles in perspective: "Remember," they say, "you are among the rare people in this world, who have electricity and indoor plumbing. You are among the educated elite, who can read and write effectively. You don't go to bed hungry, you are not dying of thirst. Reflect on this."

This is stupid advice.

I do appreciate what I have been given. I'm relieved that I eat everyday. And I'm aware that water is a sacred element that gives life, and I have it running through rivers in the pipes in my home. But to tell us when we're feeling unfortunate, to think on those without: children who starve, thirst, suffer and die. Is that meant to cheer us up?

2 Days Later

Me: I feel a little better, today.

You: Just like that?

Me: Yeah, just like that.

Mid-June, 2003
The Next Trip to Taichung; Searching for Wu Hung Li

I've returned to Taichung for one last effort. Just as I did in Taipei, I've posted flyers in all the most popular locations, such as parks and night markets. I've spoken with the local police and they have run searches through their computer network. Not surprisingly, Sigung Wu has never been arrested in Taiwan, but he also never purchased a vehicle of any sort nor registered for a license of any kind.

I've admitted to myself, that as well as wanting to meet my teacher's teacher as a show of respect, a matter of family unity and a sense of curiosity, I had hoped I would be able to coax him into teaching me, during my stay in Taiwan, R.O.C. Imagine, I could remain here exploring this culture, while still learning more Seven Star Mantis that is purely from our lineage, as well.

That's not going to happen. Thus, I continue to train; possibly more than maintaining, but improving on my abilities. However, no new knowledge is gained except that which could just as easily researched back home.

It is time to venture into another realm of Kung Fu I've been curious about: Shuai-Chiao.

Promise To Myself

I'll write my books
Pages of a life unwasted
my crying, my screaming, my laughing
my battle cries
and my victorious yops.
But I'll never write of dying
for I'll never know dying.
I'll only know living,
and then I'll know dead.

Shuai-Chiao

I've learned something else. Shuai-Chiao is not just a sport variation of Kung Fu systems. It is a Kung Fu system by itself. The sport is just a derivative created many years ago, to test each others abilities, to promote the art, and, of course, to have some fun. This was taught to me a few months ago, when I decided to research it more closely.

I've decided to study the art, as (pardon my conceit) I'm obviously a natural. I haven't written much on it until now. Suspecting it may be just a passing curiosity rather than something to which I may devote myself. I love it. Not the deep, all encompassing love that still binds me to Praying Mantis, but it is not a passing fancy.

I began my training with David Cheung, but left his class to study under Roger Soo, director and Vice-president of the International Shuai-Chiao Association. David Cheung is skilled and knowledgeable instructor, but Sifu Soo's teaching methods more closely resembles Sifu Simon's and my own. Hence, I'm much more in tune with him and better able to learn.

*   *   *   *

Like Chin Na, Shuai-Chiao doesn't have a discernable origin or a single founder. It, too, has developed over time. Earliest accounts place its origin back to 2697 B.C. It is told that the army of the Yellow Emperor, (Huang Di) Qing Shi Huang, used Shuai-Chiao to defeat all rival armies; thereby unifying China for the first time.

In the last century, the most prominent figure in Shuai-Chiao history has been Chang Tung Sheng.

Considered to be Grandmaster of the system, Chang was undefeated champion, and pioneered the spread of Shuai-Chiao to the global community. It was Grandmaster Chang, who established the training for military and police in Taiwan, as well as, writing the textbook used by those institutes. He passed on in 1985.

Grandmaster Chang had a few students. The most recognized are my instructor, Roger Soo, Gene Chicione, president of the International Shuai-Chiao Association, the founder of the American Association, Dr. Daniel Weng, and Chang's grandson, David Cheung.

All wonderful instructors, who, unfortunately, don't speak much. There is some friction among them these days, as happens in many families. I don't concern myself with social or political happenstances of this situation. I am comfortable knowing the friction will dissipate with time, if not with that generation, than the next. Sifu Cheung's leading students are pleasant men with whom I get along well. Dr. Weng's son, Jen-Yu is a gentleman, warrior and exceptional athlete. On those occasions we are able to meet and speak, it is always with sincere friendliness. Should we ever be in the same city for more than a few hours without school responsibilities to tie us down, I suspect we'd have a chance to enjoy a beer together and become real friends.

The torch has already been passed to Jen-Yu. He is President of The U.S. organization. Should I take on a similar role within our organization we will not unite the groups, but no doubt renew our connections to each other through greater communication and co-hosting of ceremonies and events… at least, that's how I see the future.

Disclaimer

Of course, my continued commitment to the International Shuai-Chiao Association is dependent on Sifu Simon's acceptance of it. I have no reason to think I wouldn't have his blessing to make the Wu Shen Temple Kung Fu Association a representative member of the International Shuai-Chiao Association. Prior to my departure from Canada, he asked me if I would like to coach Shuai-Chiao and San Shou to students that are interested. "This could be done outside our usual class schedule," he said.

Nevertheless, even after Sifu Simon semi-retires and has me and my brothers take over the school in his stead, such decisions will be dependent on his acceptance. My loyalty is first and foremost to him.

There it is.
I almost missed it.
Framed in grey, neglected,
urbanite cement.
Mountainside billowing
the green and earthen
"friends of winter"
in a land that knows only
Spring, Summer, Fall
soong, ju, mai bask proudly.
Beyond my scope
is a temple I've seen, before.
Symbolic, majestic
When I'm far enough removed
to escape the chipped paint,
gum-wrappers, and cigarette butts.

There he is.
I almost missed him.
3 right turns; street to lane to alley to pond,
in the short grass, on the bank
half-hidden by a pointed hat,
posed in *chan*-meditation;
fishing pole awaiting a remote possibility
hours,
  hours,
   hours...
I'm guessing
(hoping)

There she is.
I almost missed her.
Lotus blossom in a city skirt.
A lady
smoothed and polished
into refinement and charm
by the tongue and shell of the remnants of her ancient culture,
her oyster.
Eastern yin
  Western yang
enough to still the heart and belly
of her shaolin cowboy.

There it is. All of it. Hidden deeper than before.

This poem came to me, just in time. I will be sending it to my mother for her birthday, tomorrow.

Dear Mom,
I've been here two and a half years, now.
And I think, next week
I will run out of the toothpaste
you packed in my suitcase,
before I left.
Please send more
Love,
Jay

Early November, 2003

Years ago, my ol' pal Simon moved to England. We maintained closeness despite the distance. Recently, he and his girlfriend, Lucy came to visit. Just 10 days for us to make the most of.

We left right away for Hong Kong. I wasn't particularly interested in going, having been there a few times already. I'd hoped Thailand would be a possibility, but Si wasn't able to give me enough advanced warning to schedule a longer trip.

Small matter; Hong Kong was superb. I'm not certain which I preferred most: the spectacular view from Victoria Peak, the inspirational giant brass Buddha, or the Outback Steak House.

The company, more than anything else, made it so grand. It's too rare that Simon and I are together anymore. I think I enjoyed sitting in the hotel room having a pint before we embarked on or daily and nightly plans, as much as I did carrying out those plans.

When we returned to Taipei, I went back to work for a couple of days, expecting Simon and Lucy to explore such sights as the National Palace Museum and Chiang Kai Shek Memorial Hall Park. Instead, they slept. Sometimes you just have to do what your body tells you.

With only a short time left, I had a hell of a time deciding where to take them next: Sho Mountain, Toroko Gorge, Alishan, Green Island. Remembering that England is scarce on good beaches and good weather, I took them to Ken-Ting, a beach resort town. Can you imagine anything better than four friends resting and playing in the sun, surf and sand?

Si and I sat back in a beach shack café called Amy's Cuchina, as the girls skipped back to the motel to try on their new outfits. We gazed across a sunny day to the table-top mountain in the distance. With beer in our hands and sand on our feet, we questioned whether we could accept this Jimmy Buffet-lifestyle. Maybe not. Maybe every simple day blending into the next without any obligations would grow too empty, even with a close friend by your side. Maybe, but it's hard to imagine how long that would take.

Ten days expired and we said our sad goodbyes with happy optimism. They could have stayed with me for ten months, if they wanted.

In the Hospital… again.

I wrote my journal entry and this summary while in the hospital last night. My back injury seemed to be healing fine, until I was cleaning my apartment. I bent over the centre table to pick something up and SNAP... I was on the ground. I crawled to the phone, called my girlfriend. I couldn't even sit properly in a taxi, so we had to get an ambulance to the hospital. Sabrina stayed with me all night. Bless her heart.

I know even this shit is apart of life, but it doesn't feel like it. It feels like an interruption to life.

No doubt, stress is a major factor here. That's a vicious cycle.
Being stuck on a hospital bed while I've got so much to do causes more stress. Stress slows down the healing and so on and so on.

"Every problem has a solution" has helped me in the past. Even now, I'm writing in order to make use of what would be time wasted.

It's been 9 hours.
The physical pain is still here.
I tried to focus past it, and I still come up with mostly frustration.

Nevertheless, I'm feeling a lot of love for the woman here beside me, whose sleeping with her head on her folded arms on the end table. She should have gone home hours ago.

This journal is part of a larger story: that story being that Taiwan has shitty hospital care... Tonight, I miss Canada in a different way.

I'm certain this journal entry and the profanity within it, is showing the uglier side of me. I'm not even sure what I'm writing. I'm angry, in pain, chock full of Demerol... I can't even be sure I'm making sense.

The Waves of Life

Christmas wasn't anything like last year, but at least I took the day off work. Even an ocean away from the west I've been feeling the hustle and bustle of the holiday season. I prefer a slower pace, but I've been able to keep up.

This semester's university course is completed and I've managed to maintain my A average. Work is going well. Shuai-Chiao training is going well, too.

Sifu Roger, my training partner, Jay Romans and I went down to the town of Ping Tung to meet other instructors, whom Sifu Roger instructs and administrates. While there, I fought some exhibition matches and thumped two former Taiwan Champions. Of course, shortly afterwards, Sifu Roger proceeded to tell me how sloppy I looked. Same shit, different Sifu.

My Mantis training has suffered a little. The kid's Kung Fu class I teach at the elementary school allows me only a moment a week to review my forms.

I've been writing. I've been working out. And I've been meditating regularly. Although I'm still no expert on meditation, the calmness that finds me brings me happiness. I don't believe I would feel like a true warrior without meditation to center me, to bring into myself. It connects me to who I am supposed to be.

Surf's up.

I'm beginning to remember who I am.

"If a man dwells on the past, he robs the present, but if a man ignores the past, he may rob the future."

- Ancient Shaolin Adage

With Chinese New Year upon me, I play Janus once again. Janus was the Roman god who stood at the gate and looked both into the past and into the future. The future is, I remind myself, as it should be. It is, I remind myself further, as I must accept it -unknown.

The past is perception. Some of which I've captured in these pages. As I reread them I laugh at myself. Happiness is written here; and the reasons for it are insignificant. It needs no reason. It needs only to exist.

Also included here are complaints and frustrations. Here is where most of the humour lies. I notice that each one is a product of attachment or a concern that I don't have enough time. And time is just another attachment, really.

I laugh recognizing that I am so far from enlightenment. It stands ahead of me, a thousand miles a way. Just as it stands one step forward. Maybe someday I'll let go of my fear and take that step.

*   *   *

The Buddha, Padmasambhava, said, "The nature of everything is open… Even though it is the thing that is most essentially yours, you seek for it elsewhere. How amazing."

The Buddha, Jesus Christ said, "Ask for it and ye shall receive, seek and ye shall find."

Lao Tzu said, "When you seek it, you will not find it."

I believe when you understand how it is that they are all saying the same thing, you have taken your first big step towards awakening.

January 22nd, 2004

It's the 2nd night of the Chinese New Year celebration. In the small town of Jiow Shi, Sabrina and I sit in a hot-spring. After dusk, through the mild darkness, a few lights press through tall, dry grass and bamboo, creating dark hypnotic images. These shadows, these incorrigible bachelors entice the hot-spring steam to dance. They sway together playfully before us, like flirtatious ghosts.

Were it solitary and soundless, the scene might be gothic. As it is, Sabrina and I can also see beyond the bamboo and past the rice fields to the festival less than two acres away. Town folk walk about the food stands and games. A fountain whose brightly coloured abstract structure stands 30 feet high, has waterspouts around it which spray just as high. A disco ball, ill-placed but eye-catching, spins atop it. Cheesy '80's love songs play loud enough for us to enjoy… or not enjoy depending on your opinion of Jack Wagner, Billy Ocean and Wham. I'm not a fan, but it's soft and low and able to lull us into a relaxed romantic peace. Our bodies lean on each other and our skin welcomes the therapeutic minerals of the hot water.

The Fever

Coach Hong of the Taipei Expert Wrestling Team finally convinced me to compete. The Taipei Wrestling Championships are being held April 1st. I said I'd do it… and, upon agreeing, the fever struck me as it did years ago.

I'd thought I'd rid myself of it back then. After 8 years of wrestling, at the age of 21, I'd thought I'd outgrown it. When I entered the U.S. Shuai-Chiao Kung Fu Championships in 1998, it wasn't the fever. It was just showing a little pride in our school - a demonstration of our training. I took second place that year… and the year after that. Once I tasted competition again, the fever was upon me. In fact, in those two years, I also took the Bronze in the Pan-American Games for San Shou (Chinese Kickboxing) and the bronze at the Canadian Pankration Championships. *Always a bridesmaid, never a bride.*

After finally achieving the gold in 2000, I thought it best to retire from sport-fighting as a champ at the age of 30. The fever had broken.

Now, four years later, I've stepped up my training, I'm sparring again and I'm lifting more weight than ever before, because I can smell victory just a few weeks away. I'm itching to prove a guy in his mid-thirties can do it.

The Contradiction

This desire seems to me to be juxtaposed to the philosophies I embrace.
Am I abiding in the Tao?
Am I dissolving my desires when I strive for victory?
Am I awakening to the truth?
I'm going to seek out some of the local monks and ask their opinions on this state of mind.

The Setback

Sifu Roger took us to the Police College to train with another instructor and the cadets. No stretching followed our warm-ups, so we went straight into sparring. I should have voiced my objection, despite being a guest in the training hall.

I tore my hamstring.

The tournament is only two weeks away. My calmness is only a front; inside I'm angry with myself. I don't want to give it up. Maybe I won't, but for the last couple of weeks I had unshakable confidence. This rip in my muscle is a tear in my confidence, as well.

The Victory

Yup, I won.

How?

The Zone

This explanation might be helpful for athletes:

Throughout high school, I strove to be a wrestling champion. On a low level I succeeded. With diligent training and fortitude I became the Southern Ontario Wrestling Champ 5 years straight. But on a higher level, Provincial Championships, I never placed higher than third. I had always managed to prove myself to be the worst of the best, never better.

When I began competing again, in '98 and '99, I encountered the same problem. I had no explanation why. It wasn't for lack of training. It wasn't for lack of heart. Hours and hours of studying great athletes had taught me what was needed to be a champion. I knew how to be in the zone. Or did I?

As a teen, my nearest sport-fighting role model was Dave Beneteau. In getting psyched up, Dave became like a machine. A switch turned on and he was in serious destruction mode. Many great athletes are similar; "No nonsense; let's get down to business. I've got a job to do and nobody stands in my way." Boxers Rocky Marcianno, and Marvelous Marvin Haggler were this way. Basketball legend, Larry Bird was all about no nonsense efficiency, as is David Beckham on the soccer field and Pete Sampras on the tennis court.

I tried for years to be the same way. When the big matches came, I was pumped… and I lost, anyway.

How could it be so? I had the same mentality going into those championships as those other guys. So what failed me?

I studied video footage of myself and it became clear as crystal. No athlete wants to admit to himself that he chokes when the pressure is on, but there it was. In my earlier matches I was loose and free and in the finals I was stiff and rigid.

I wasn't in the place I wanted to be. I wasn't in the zone.

I continued studying footage of great sport-fighters, but this time from a different perspective. Instead of analyzing techniques, I began analyzing attitude; trying to gain insight into their different psyches.

I began to notice that when performing at their best, different athletes demonstrate different personality traits. It hit me: **The zone is a different place for each different person.**

This realization was a major breakthrough for me. I could see that Mohammed Ali was in a different place than Rocky Marcianno. Sugar Ray Leonard was in a different place than Marvelous Marvin. And I needed to be in a different place than my ol' pal, Dave.

Some athletes are machines, but others are more like showboats. Not because they disrespect their opponents, but because that's what they need to win. I am in the latter group… less Larry Bird and more Michael Jordan, less Beckham and more Pele.

From that point on, every time I practiced or visualized myself competing, I pictured myself having fun. I didn't need to win before I could celebrate. I would celebrate my victory as it was happening.

For years they called me The Cowboy, but I suppose I looked more like a rodeo clown the year I won. In previous years I let out an occasional cheer and a swing of my hips only in the early matches. In the year 2000, I lived up to my nickname, I whooped and hollered like a cowboy. I danced and pranced and shook my ass all the way to victory.

On April 1st of this year, given an opportunity to remind myself how that feels, I again played as much as I fought my way to a gold medal. I even defeated a former national champion to do it.

The Fever (reprise)

It hasn't burned out of me just yet. Not one week later, I've been invited to compete in another event in which to test my mettle: the first ever Asia Pacific Rim Jiu-Jitsu Championships. Although, I've never studied or competed in Jiu-jitsu I hope to attend. More so, I'm setting my sights on the World Shuai-Chiao Championships… if they ever get organized. One thing I've learned about Chinese culture, is that it has a severe lack of organization. Nevertheless, I'll do my best to be prepared. I'll be certain to have fun, and hell, I might even win… provided I still have the fever and I can carry it to the zone.

The Defeat

There's nothing like defeat to clip your ego and put things in perspective.

It came at the Asia Pacific Rim Jiu-jitsu Championships. Six Pacific Rim Countries were represented, as well as combatants from New Zealand, Australia, Canada and the U.S. Although there were a lot of countries represented the tournament mostly consisted of beginners, low intermediate and high intermediate competitors. The black belt category held only 3 competitors, of which I was one. The conveners tried to convince me not to compete at that level. They felt that since I had no experience in Jiu-jitsu tournaments, it would be an unfair disadvantage for me. They should have been more concerned about the disadvantage in weight. As it turned out, there were no fighters in the middle-weight category, so I fought as a heavyweight. My opponent, Steve Kamphurios was about 70 pounds heavier than me. As well, Steve had been a world champion (in the over-30 age division) in Jiu-jitsu.

The defeat wasn't heart wrenching.

Despite Steve's size advantage and experience in the sport, he wasn't able to score on me. By his own admission, "you've got great footwork. I was frustrated because I couldn't throw you."

Half way through the match, I was winning, but then Steve pulled off a brilliant move. Setting me up to believe he was doing a sacrificial judo roll, I countered by stepping out and reached through his legs. He was actually setting up an arm bar, which he executed while upside down. I tapped out.

I was surprised at how much praise I received from this loss. A lot of people were talking about me before the match; terms like "crazy" were used mostly. But many of those same people openly changed their tune after they saw my performance.

On the one hand, I'm disappointed. On the other hand, I gave that heavyweight champion a hell of a match.

May 29th,

I've rested and rested. All my injuries are just about recovered. I feel awful.

These weeks of resting have left me feeling soft and weak. I've often had people ask me how I find time to train, but I can't understand how people don't train. Is this how most people feel all the time?

I resumed my running a few days ago. I felt completely lop-sided. Even at a slow pace, my right side can't keep up with my left. Yesterday, I tried a couple short sprints. My left leg had so much more spring than the right, I almost ran in circles.

I feel nothing like a warrior… today.

'TIME', I remind myself, 'TIME'.

June 5th, 2004

With my focus returning to more traditional training, I question my return to the realm of combat sports. Certainly, there is much to be gained by indulging in the spirit of competition. However, with each moment that my mind indulges in a vision of victory, I may be pulling myself further from the true nature of my mind, the Tao (what Buddhists call "awakening"). It seems to be one step forward and two steps back, or maybe, more optimistically, two forward and one back.

I am told we subconsciously fear awakening. Many elements make us fearful: we fear a loss of comfort with the familiar, we fear a loss of ego, which has convinced us of its necessity, we fear a loss of self, that our individuality will slip away, which is, really the two fore-mentioned fears combined.

But there is another fear: one which I've never heard addressed. The fear that I believe is the greatest obstacle between my current state and the awakening. That is the fear of the loss of fun.

Consider it: if we rid ourselves of desires, do we not rid ourselves of goals? Goals, even like athletic championships, can be fun in both their pursuit and their capture. This realization makes wonder what other fun might be sacrificed in the search for enlightenment. How much fun? Do I want to let go of that?

Thailand

I just got back from Thailand. It was mostly a great trip. Thailand is better than Taiwan in some ways. In Taiwan you can find some traditional culture, but you really need to dig for it.

The Thai, on the other hand, revel in their culture. When we walked into our hotel lobbies, doormen where dressed in traditional costumes and beautiful Thai women were playing traditional instruments in specified postures. Even very new buildings have the old style design for their roofs. There are giant temples, and shrines all over the place. Everywhere you turn there is some kind of performance demonstrating Thai culture.

There's almost as many cultural performances as there are she-male burlesque shows (i.e. drag-queens).

WARNING: if you are a single man and in Thailand be very, very careful; even sober, some of these guys were beautiful... you cannot tell the difference...better than anyone you've seen on Jerry Springer...it's quite disturbing!

On a different note; we also spent some time with wild animals. We played with elephants at a safari park, met orangutans, a bear and a leopard... I even nursed a baby tiger. Most of these animals had plenty of experience with people. The most wild were on this small, uninhabited island. Sabrina and I, along with some other people, rented a boat on our way to a secluded isle where we were to spend the day playing on the beach. We stopped at this smaller island where monkeys could be seen along the shore and in the trees; dozens of them.

I was sharing a banana with a small one, when I suggested that Sabrina take a picture. She got out her camera and shortly after he ran off with what was left of our banana, she asked, "When do you want me to take a photo?"

I quipped, "Damn, it's a good thing you're pretty."

Leaving Cambridge

After a year and a half, I take my leave. More than a dozen other teachers are going, as well.

This extravagant private school has first class facilities, a breathtaking view and the teachers I worked with, both foreign and Taiwanese, were top notch. Not only were they fine educators but great people to sit and enjoy a pint with after work.

I leave because of the administration. I could no longer stomach the incompetence, stubbornness, and racism of the majority of the administrative staff. They took what could have been the best school in Taiwan and ran it like a cheap cram school.

Allow me one example: despite reminders from the foreign language department that procrastination would cause problems, the administration failed to order the proper amount of textbooks for each class. For over a month, we were teaching without the required textbooks. As a result, we were making many photocopies to provide the students with the material or reasonable substitutes.

Administration, seeing the increase in photocopies suddenly, and without warning, put a restriction on or photocopies cards. One day, several of us discovered we could not make any photocopies for the rest of the month. Now we had no textbooks or handouts to provide the students.

At our next staff meeting we asked why. We were told quite clearly that administration was aware that we had been making an unusually large amount of copies and so deduced that the foreign teachers were illegally copying school texts for our moonlighting teaching job… or possibly for our own private schools which we were undoubtedly planning to organize.

Just an ordinary day at Cambridge.

The final straw came at the end of the year when it was time to renew our contracts. Although there was no mention of the many events we organized above the call of our contracts, nor any gratitude shown for developing a curriculum (which was originally the administration's responsibility), we did receive some praise for our teaching. For all our hard work, we were being rewarded with an offer to pay us less money per hour.

Goodbye Cambridge.

I'm going to miss many of my co-workers, even one or two good apples in the administration's rotten bunch. Several of the people I've gotten to be friends with are leaving the country.

Matt and Dave are staying in Taiwan but live in the far reaches of the county. I'm not certain how often I'll be able to hang out with them. Beth is heading back to the U.S., Gordon and his family are moving to the Philippines. Ray's wife has been temporarily transferred to Shanghai. They'll be there at least a year.

Even Shaun Corrigan, our head teacher, a nine year veteran of Taiwan is heading home to South Africa. Shaun, or 'Oh Captain, my Captain' as I sometimes referred to him, is a warrior. I'm not referring to the staff room battles he fought time and time again to insure the kids were getting the education to which they were entitled. Nor do I refer to enduring the attacks of office politics, which threatened the teachers' reputations and integrity.

In his younger days in South Africa, Shaun led one of the organizations in the fight against apartheid. Most often, words were his weapons but the protesters often had violent opposition. Thus Shaun has proven himself a warrior in a much more literal sense.

The night I said goodbye to our captain, he gave me a gift to symbolize our friendship. It reflects the discussions on warriorship we shared. It was a Mabiti war-stick. It is an archaic weapon of the Mabiti tribe, which inhabits the lands around the South Africa-Zimbabwe border.

For all I know, this may be common stock for any South African or Zimbabwe flea market. But I treasure it, because to me it represents an acknowledgment from a warrior I respect.

Death

I saw a man die today.

I don't know a better way to start this journal entry. I don't want to build up to it. I just want to get it out there.

My friend, Frank, his wife, Yi-Shen, Sabrina and I went to a windy beach. Frank is teaching us to kite-surf. We sat in the SUV eating a snack before embarking. We looked up and saw a guy down in the sand with a woman and a small boy next to him. Earlier was splashing about in the waves. At first we thought he must have hurt his leg or something, but a couple of other people got closer so we tore on down the beach to see what the situation was. A big foreign guy was giving him mouth to mouth and they were trying CPR. I yelled to I-Shen to call 119 (Taiwan's emergency number, i.e. 911). But the ambulance took a hell of a long time... not that it mattered... he had no chance. Maybe if there had been a lifeguard rescue unit with the proper equipment on hand, AS THERE SHOULD HAVE BEEN ... but even then, I can't say for sure. We turned him upside down and a gallon of water rushed out.

You stand there waiting and waiting for him to come around, denying what you know is true, until finally you realize he's not going to come around.

It was the first time I'd watched someone die. It was awful. And I've never felt so useless in my whole life. I know I've heard people say this before, but now I understand it; it's strange that there's no noise when it happens... no angels, no trumpets, just dead.

The water he drowned in was only waist high. It turns out he was a rookie to kite-surfing and he couldn't swim... we also found out he was very drunk... in a nutshell, he died from stupidity.

I thought seeing something like that was supposed to change a person in some way, but I don't feel changed.

Paiwan

Earlier I said, "if you want to find traditional culture in Taiwan, you really have to dig for it." I should have said, "if you want to find traditional *Chinese* culture…" The same isn't true of the aboriginal people. They are happy to show off their customs and festivals.

Recently, Sifu Roger and I went down to an aboriginal village near Ping Tung City, with his good friend Sifu Yu. Sifu Yu is an elder in the Paiwan tribe, as well as a Shuai-Chiao kung fu instructor. The Paiwan tribe had a festival the day before our Shuai-Chiao seminar was to be held at the local high school. Sifu Yu introduced us to the local people and invited us to attend the celebration.

In the town community centre we talked with the local natives, drank barley wine and played with the local children. Later, we ventured around the village introducing ourselves to the town folk celebrating in front of their houses.

The term village may conjure images that don't suit the modern day. Most houses and stores were humble shacks, but were nevertheless constructed of modern materials, mortar and aluminum. Occasionally, wood and bamboo would be used, as well. There is no polite way for me to tell you these dwellings were ugly. Even the community center resembled nothing more than a brick vending stand with a crude basketball court in the middle of a dirt lot.

We eventually came across a more luxurious looking abode, where we were invited to partake in more barley wine. The owner, I soon discovered was the tribal chief. I suppose I should have guessed this from his Rolex. It turned out that the music celebration had been delayed because the chief, who was to host the event, had gotten drunk and passed out. I don't want to paint him as an irresponsible cultural leader. In fact, others assured me that he was ordinarily quite dignified. This was simply an unusual side-effect of the merriment of the occasion. And since it was constant visiting of his people that drove him to his intoxication, they were not only forgiving, but downright amused by it.

I was thrilled to take part in the music and dancing, which began four hours late. Time constraints don't appear to be apart of the Paiwan philosophy.

September, 2004

Recently, my training and meditation has been restricted to my living room. Day after day the rain has come. Earlier I'd mentioned how purging and regenerating the rain can be. My buddy, Kev agrees that the rain can feel spiritually purging when it unexpectedly drops in on his training. Kev trains for triathlons. Endurance training also helps him with his rock-climbing. He is currently ranked 6th in Ontario despite being in his mid-thirties.

Knowing it affects me the same way, you would think that I would eagerly welcome each cloud burst as a moment to join in nature's dance with reckless abandon. Not so. Today I stood in the doorway tentatively eyeing the cold pins of water showering down, tensed my muscles at the thought of their tiny bites and took a long moment to prepare myself.

Then I went. Walking slowly to the park, hoping that as my skin grew wetter it would adjust. It eventually did.

At the park, I resumed my dance with nature, relishing the energy the rain gave to my Kung Fu forms. Later, as I practiced my chi cultivation with my eyes closed, I could feel drops passing through my circles of energy. I sat in meditation for an hour and then stood and walked home. All the while, trusting that my refined spiritual energy would keep me healthy.

I'm sick, today.

Go ahead, laugh it up.

Shugyo (Nov.13, 2004)

My shoulder injury reduced my maximum bench press by 10 lbs., but my running time is faster than it was two years ago. I even began with an impressive 100m dash this year. The rope skipping and plyometrics, which followed the five-mile run, darn near killed me. I managed to get through 21 of 24 forms without any mistakes. Of course, I also added my shuai-chiao patterns to my agenda. My exhausted body began to influence my mind. On three forms I made small mistakes. Answers, which would normally sail from my tongue, were now a struggle to find and pry from my tired brain. But I got through it and felt like a better man for it.

Unfortunately, no strong celebration followed. Sabrina and I opted for a quiet evening at home. I don't want to abuse my body through the customary birthday celebration. Next weekend, I'm attending a major Shuai-Chiao seminar; I don't know what it will entail.

The Seminar

Two days, 10 hours a day of classroom lectures and gym time. Not only Shuai-Chiao techniques were discussed, but teaching philosophies, nutrition, sport injury prevention and healing, biomechanics and mathematics were lectured on. Some were fairly basic lessons and others were pretty weighty stuff; all of it difficult when Chinese isn't your first language.

A Step in the Right Direction

I've been studying Reflexology and Herbalism for about six weeks, so far. I thought they would be good precursors to my study of acupuncture. I'm picking up Reflexology quickly. The academics of it are interesting enough to absorb without much effort. The practical application has some easy points and some more difficult techniques. I'm practicing often to improve them and reading volumes of texts in both fields.

I am very pleased with myself that I am finally doing serious study in healing people after 22 years of learning to drop them.

Not Just Another Christmas Overseas

Howie and his girlfriend, Vivian; Dave Kinsella, his wife Pearl, and their baby girl, Meagan; Frank Nieve and his wife, Yi-Shen; Sabrina and I spent Christmas together at my place.

Despite any other accomplishments you may have heard me brag about, yesterday's achievement was my grandest: Christmas dinner. I made Shepard's Pie, layers of mashed potatoes vegetables and ground beef topped with gravy-for me this was feat divinely inspired. The turkey was store bought and prepared. My guests were pleased with the meal, the wine and the popping of the after dinner Christmas crackers. It wasn't a perfect Christmas, but we almost captured that down home feel.

Monday Dec. 27th, 2004

A major earthquake happened yesterday in the ocean of the coast of Thailand. It measured 9.0 on the Richter scale. As well as shaking several buildings into rubble, it caused a tidal wave reportedly 10 metres high. One should understand that those waves do not break. This wall of water advanced inward overtaking waterfront cities and entire islands belongings to Thailand, Malaysia, and India. So far, about 25,000* people have been found dead.

Are the people around me experiencing the grief? Are they sensitive enough to grieve for strangers or am I simply transferring my sorrow on to the faces I see about me?

It would be easy on these grey dismal sunless days to mistake their solemn expressions for mourning.

I suppose I hope they are.

My studies and practice carry the idea that all life is connected and that we have an inner force that others can feel, some can even see. Shouldn't I have felt any icy shiver or a tight grip on insides giving us some clue that thousands of people had lost their lives in one moment? Shouldn't that many lives ending in such a short space of time caused some sort of shockwave or some sort of void that the bio-energies of the rest of us would rush to fill?

"I felt a strange disturbance in the force; like millions of voices cried out in pain and then were suddenly silenced"

Obi Wan Kenobi
-Star Wars (A New Hope)

I hope quoting Alec Guinness' memorable character doesn't appear trite or comical. I think I was expecting to feel something as profound as what he describes. As I am just a novice in the field of human energies, I suppose that's too much to expect. Nevertheless, something has affected me and others around me. I had a conversation with Sabrina this morning. We both mentioned a restless night wherein bad dreams woke us up several times. At work two of my coworkers described their nights the same way. At the time, having not yet heard about the tragedy, I dismissed it as a result of the full moon. In retrospect, though the moon has the power to disturb our sleep, I've never thought of it as a negative energy.

Perhaps the massive tragedy did have resonance rippling around the globe. I just didn't know how to read it.

*By January 2nd, 2005 it had been released that at least 127,000 lives had been lost.

What Seems Surreal

I have tried to be honest in my writings. Even after I realized that I was writing for an audience, my intent has been to be completely raw. However, I can't deny that I have held back those aspects of my training and cultivation which may seem too surreal. Most often a writer will take 'poetic license'; a sly way of saying we will lie to sell our books. I am guilty of the opposite – not wanting to sound far-fetched. Here is some of what I've been denying my readers:

When I began training in Chi cultivation, not only did I feel a stirring in my dan tien that unsettled me, and an energy winding through the meridians of my body, my mind, too, was affected. I woke up one morning to an eye staring back at me. That, of course, was odd. Odd, but not startling. This eye was close to my forehead. It was a black and white image and it was moving. Everywhere I shifted my focus, the eye would move, as well. If I tried to look down to examine the lower part of the eye, the eye would also look down with perfect synchronization.

I then realized that I couldn't see anything else but the eye. Only then did it occur to me that my eyes were closed. 'Well, that explains it,' I thought, 'My eyes are closed because I'm not really awake yet. I'm dreaming.'

So, I opened them. There was my pillow. I turned over. There was my alarm clock, the wall and the window. I continued to turn. There was the ceiling. I was most definitely awake. I closed my eyes again. The eye in the middle of my forehead was still there in shades of grey. After continuing to shift my focus and having the eye mirror my efforts for several seconds, it dawned on me. This eye wasn't mirroring my movements. It was my eye! I was directing it.

But all it could do was look back at itself. I was confused. If this was my so-called third eye, it seemed pretty useless.

I later learned from John Hong that this was indeed my third eye, but that it had not yet "turned". Thus it was, and still is, unable to reveal anything to me.

On another morning shortly there after, I awoke with an image in my mind. This image was clear in detail, strong and lasting. I couldn't shake it. This image so imbedded in my mind was… a street corner (take a moment to let that sink in)… Not the face of Jesus, not a burning bush, not Bodiharma, not Vishnu or the Raven. No scared temple, Stone Henge, Mount Olympus, or the rings of Saturn… just a street corner.

My perspective was diagonally across from a shop, looking up slightly so that part of the shop's sign was revealed. Only the sign had colour; red words on a yellow sign. The rest of the image was black and white. What did the words say? I don't know. I couldn't read any Chinese at the time.

What's more, the image was backwards. How do I know? A day later, in the real world, I saw it. Standing on a corner, I looked up and saw the image in reverse, in full colour.

At this point, you should be awaiting the climax of the story: because I was looking at the sign something incredible took place and I was able to save someone's life or maybe my own.

I'm sorry. I have no such highlight to offer you. Nothing happened. All this premonition told me was that I would be at that spot.

Another minor phenomenon occurred. I began to see things: sentient beings all about. According to my research these beings have always been with us; living in this realm but in a slightly differently tuned dimensional phase. In recent centuries we have lost our ability to see them. In my case, the only beings I could see were small bug-like creatures. Perhaps, I should say more like crayfish. Most often they were white, but occasionally other colours. Climbing strands of air as though they were tangible columns.

I couldn't communicate with them. I'm not a shaman - not yet, if ever. Once in the Fu Da University gym, I saw a larger entity. A shadowman was watching me practice Kung Fu. I say "man" because 'he' had a masculine presence. On this occasion I sensed some rapport. He was applauding me. I didn't feel as though he was overly impressed by me. It was more like the favourable support one gets from a parent or an encouraging teacher. Something else came through; as if he was telling me it was alright to take greater physical risks, to try more dangerous techniques, the world keeps me safe. I don't know how an intangible being, who thus far appealed immobile, intended to spot me. Nevertheless, I engaged in some wall running and back flips.

If I tell you I took a year hiatus from my more advanced chi cultivation, you'll no doubt question why.

Why would I stop doing something that had such significant effect? I'm not really certain myself. Oh, I have excuses, but not real reasons.

After my initiation with John Hong, I began practicing at Sun Yet San Memorial Hall Park with a small group. These fellow practitioners were a friendly lot, but unreliable. Several Saturdays I would show up and find myself alone. Still, any chi development is not contingent on other people.

I had several distractions but nothing which should have been strong enough to lure me away from this magnificent esoteric exercise.

In truth, I don't know exactly what force was involved in deterring me from this life-enhancing ritual. I only suspect that it was more than the basic sloth of modern man. Each time I try to begin the ritual I was overcome with feelings of illness and fatigue.

A few months ago, I finally came to my senses. I worked through the headaches, upset stomachaches, drowsiness and burning eyes, which obstructed my efforts. I just did it any way. Eventually the symptoms left me. For five months, now I have been back on the path.

There were no noticeable results at first; it was three months before I even felt an improvement in my energy. When that began to improve, the animals began to approach me as they had before.

When I meditate in a park or deeper wilderness, animals cautiously get closer to me. I have always had an affinity for animals. As a child, I had a couple of occasions when wild birds allowed me to lift them up. I touched squirrels, played with snakes and once even hand fed a wild raccoon.

Only later was I told these things are dangerous. As a 'logical' adult, I confine myself more to relationships with domestic animals. Even these are sometimes unusual. For example, a group of people leaning on the wooden fence of a corral trying to gain a horse's attention would look surprised when the horse would dismiss them and canter over to me, standing apart from the group.

Once in New Brunswick, my friends, Sheilagh, Eddie and I entered a garage adjoined to a house where a local tattoo artist had his home studio. A large German shepherd growled as we went in. I squatted down and tilted my head. He then bounded off the step at me and was soon licking my face.

The artist's wife entered the garage to warn us. "Stay away from the dog, he doesn't like… Oh," she cut herself off. "That's strange; he usually bites strangers if they get too close."

Incidents such as these are common for me. So, small creatures approaching me during my stillness in the woods did not seem unusual.

A meditation teacher explained to me that what is in fact happening, is that the animals are trying to steal my chi. They sense it and are drawn to it. This is not something to be alarmed about because the chi transference is reciprocal. It circulates between the meditator and the animals. Circulating chi is healthy chi.

Of course, the animals don't know this. At least I've never known any one who suspects they do. They merely want to take the chi, just as they would snatch peanuts from a pile.

Now a couple of months later, I am seeing more than woodland creatures. The smaller silent beings are beginning to become visible again.

January 2nd, 2005

My spiritual training is bringing depth to my awareness. My social-interactive gift of being able to read people and to accurately empathize with them is developing into a stronger intuition.

I think my dreams are being affected. They've become strange allegorical stories of my relations with other people and the world. I'm usually aware they are dreams and able to control them. Usually, but not always; one night I bolted upright in bed trying to pull the centipedes out from under my skin. One morning I woke up heart-broken that I had killed a man in self-defense.

An interesting thing about my dreams is that I'm now able to read in them. This is something I once thought was impossible… that whole right brain, left brain thing.

Often I converse with ghosts, demons, animal spirits and occasionally a live person who has wondered into my dream realm.

It's been exciting and sometimes entertaining. But I don't feel as though I've been getting enough sleep.

My dreams have been telling me that something is troubling Sifu. I've tried to call him to see if that's true, but the differing time zones have kept me from reaching him.

January 7, 2005

I've never believed myself to be one of those gifted clairvoyants whose dreams are premonitions. I still don't. But dreams can be a bridge between one time and another, one place and another, even one person and another.

When I called Sifu this morning and told him of feeling a need to call based on some dreams I had concerning his well-being, it was as if I'd gotten his message.

He said he'd be thinking of me and wanted to share some recent events. Some difficult, some laughable, some terrible.

These are not Sifu Simon's journals and I'm not a liberty to air his personal dealings publicly. It's enough for me to say that he is handling these battles with faith, strength, humour and conviction, as a true warrior is inclined to do.

Chill the Beer – Company's Comin'

Brad is arriving for Chinese New Year. I'm pretty excited…Strangely, I was a little nervous, too. He's my best friend and ordinarily when he comes to my home I don't care if there are dirty dishes in the sink and my underwear is on the floor. I don't bring him beer because he knows where the fridge is. I never try to impress him. What would be the point? I'm a dirt poor teacher and he's a wealthy engineering project manager…

We both know it. It's never been an issue in our friendship. I sometimes call him "Rockefeller".

The only reason for any concern now is that I know he worries about me. He hasn't seen anything of my life here and he believes Taiwan is a "2nd world" country. I just want him to be sure I'm not suffering over here. I suppose he'll just have to see it and feel it here. I'm happy, sometimes a little home sick, but very, very happy.

January 14, 2005

Next month it will have been 4 years since I arrived in Taiwan.

I remember when I first arrived. Every so often I would stop in mid-pace during my walk a think "Holy Smokes! I'm in Asia." That doesn't happen anymore. Still, certain places I go and certain things I see are so undeniably Asian. I suspect Brad will have that reaction when he visits. A market place where vendors scream out their deals; bargain rates for fruits, vegetables or still live creatures which flop, flutter or squirm in their bins and cages. Monumental wooden doors and colourful sweeping roofs, ornamented temples with columns carved into the complex spiral of the elongated bodies of dragons.

Locals and "lifers" don't notice them much, but newcomers invariably pause with each encounter.

On one side of Elephant mountain by my neighborhood, is a community of lavish mansions. Sabrina and I have walked that area admiring the homes. Yesterday we went a different route. On the North Eastern face of Elephant Mountain is a community quite contrary to its southern face. An assemblage of shacks and alleys, twisting and turning all about, form a mortar labyrinth. I scarcely imagine how they navigate through that neighborhood. It is step back into a previous century, where only the sight of modern address plates and the occasional washing machine give indication that the people who live there know what year it is.

If I take my buddy there, and we wind one way through this ménage of trees and antique dwellings no doubt he'll pause and I think "Holy smokes! I'm in Asia."

Feb. 15th, 2005

Brad has come and gone. I feel sad. I feel good.

His trip cost quite a few coins more than I'd planned, but I gained from it, too; not simply hazy memories of funny drunken antics, - although those were worth making.

I gained optimism. I strengthened.

I came home from the airport after watching him leave, looked about the place and thought 'Now, what… I have much to do; but not as much to look forward to'. And my own home is suddenly missing someone I prefer to have around.

There was a moment of grief that was so brief it's barely worth mentioning. Then without warning, happiness attacked and grief succumbed to it. I still have a life on the other side of the planet, where I still fit comfortably.

Now, don't misunderstand me. Comfort can be overrated. We need to make ourselves uncomfortable sometimes. Other times, it's a warm blanket on a chilly night.

Yesterday was my four year anniversary of coming to Taiwan. I've changed a lot in four years.

I've changed in good ways. Grand ways. Ways I'm quite proud of.

Returning home to Ontario means revealing those changes to the people I've grown up knowing. That should be a good thing, but people are often uncomfortable with changes.

Certainly, my friends can accept the Jay, who is more secure and mature, and the Jay who has "conquered all his adolescent fear."

But can they accept the Jay who is more spiritual; the Jay who loves solace; the Jay who finds happiness in meditation; the Jay who insists on connecting with nature as often as possible; the Jay whose emotions are on the surface; the Jay who sings out loud; that believes in the healing power of chi; that see ghosts and speaks with unseen entities, praises totems and dances in the sacred places; the Jay that is always trying to see past the illusion that they still believe in; the Jay that knows that by trying to be less animalistic, we have become less human; the Jay that's trying to be fully human again.

Yes.

Yes, they can. Oh, Brad mocks me playfully occasionally, for my way of being, but he most certainly still accepts me. And I think Kevin and Rich are not so far removed from Brad's attitude that I need worry about them.

During these four years I've come to understand things Sifu had spoken of, that I didn't really get before. I hope the pressure of conformity hasn't taken these things from him during my absence.

During these four years I've come to understand things my dad had spoken of, that I didn't really get before. I didn't expect that to happen.

Regardless of the changes, I am also still the Jay who wants to hang out in the backyard, barbecuing steaks, drinking beer with the boys. We'll talk to our women like idiot tough-guys trying to be their bosses, while they'll roll their eyes and laugh at us, for our charade.

Each of us, men and women, secure in the knowledge that not one of us would rather be anywhere else with any other people.

This has not changed. In this way, I have not changed. After Brad's ten day visit, that realization fills me with a yearning to return home.

The March in March

"Don't talk politics!" That's what we learn. We're told it's a social faux pas. Perhaps, I'm paranoid but I believe that idea was instilled into North American culture by some higher authority to keep the masses silent. I've adhered to this machination throughout my journals because most people don't like to discuss politics. Certainly people who would buy this book aren't looking for a political rant. Thus, though politics are at the foreground of so much here in Taiwan these days, I've written nothing of them.

It may be irresponsible of me not to comment after spending so much time in a country that is politically threatened.

The march I was involved in was a protest wherein about a million people marched through the heart of Taipei in defiance of China's latest inane "law". Their declaration is that they will militaristically invade Taiwan should the island nation do anything that could be perceived as an attempt to seek independence.

They are getting away this threat, as well, despite the U.S. statement that they will allow nothing which disrupts the status quo.

Most citizens of the U.S. and certainly other parts of the world are being misled as to what the status quo really is by governmentally influenced media (Most TV networks, Time magazine, etc). They say things like, "if Taiwan seeks independence" or "should Taiwan attempt to break free of China". Such phrases are deliberate attempts to deceive the public about the current situation. The situation is this: Taiwan **is** a free and independent nation, **right now**. It is not something they are seeking to change. Taiwan is not about to start a revolution. It is a sovereign country with its own government, its own military, its own system of taxation and healthcare; its own **democratically elected** president, and its own flag which it is not allowed to show at the Olympics.

The U.S. is involved, but refuses to take sides. Strange considering it was fine to change the status quo back in 1776 when the people of the United States decided they would no longer tolerate a system of government which was controlling and unfair. The whole founding of that country is supposedly to support a government of the people and for the people. This is allegedly why the American government took such a vehement stance against Communist governments after World War II.

Presently, a free nation with democratic elections is threatened by a Communist country wherein human rights are virtually non-existent. I use the term Communist loosely. China is not actually communistic, but in fact, is a tyrancy. It is a corrupt kingdom, wherein the old boys in charge believe it is their right to do whatever they please.

I mention the U.S. involvement because it has, as always, positioned itself as a key player. However, I do not solely fault the American government. The majority of the governments of the world are part of the grand hypocrisy.

Are we, the citizens of the world, to believe that any nation is prepared to defend Taiwan unless it suits their specific needs? The Nazi government took Austria and the world did nothing. China took Tibet and the world did nothing. The Nazis took Poland and Czechoslovakia and the world did nothing. If China takes Taiwan….

"If we dwell in the past, we rob the present; but if we ignore the past, we may well rob the future. The seeds of our destiny are nourished by the experiences of our past."

- Ancient Shaolin Adage*

*Yes, I know I said that earlier. I'm not ignoring the past.

Oh Canada,

Sabrina and I have decided to return to Canada. I love Taiwan. But I love Canada, too. And home in Essex County I have some dreams that have yet to see fruition. We began making plans. (Did I say "plans"?)

The government paper work is an enormous hassle. Most of it is obviously relevant. Some of it is ridiculously unnecessary. All of it is confusing.

Unfortunately, the government employees have no desire to be helpful. At the Canadian embassy, I was constantly reminded that my questions were interfering with their *real work*; whatever that might be. I reminded the stuffed shirt with whom I was dealing that he had told me to download the information and that it would be easy to understand and quick to fill out. I then presented him with the 32 pages that Sabrina and I were to sift through and attempted to draw to his attention to how confusing many of the questions and requirements are. As I tried to get some information to assist us, he repeated over and over again that it was not his job to answer my questions. Finally, I requested he find the employee whose job it is to help Canadian citizens. For a brief moment he became a real person and helped us with some questions.

Even after filling out all these forms which ask such important details as "What did Sabrina's mother study in college?" (I kid you not), we still had a lot of work to do acquiring university transcripts, health examination files, and police record checks

After this was completed and the paperwork was sent to Citizenship and Immigration Canada, the worst was still not over. We had to tell her parents.

This was a drawn out painful night. There was no hostility. They aren't racist and, in fact, are quite fond of me, but they couldn't pretend to be pleased that there little girl was going to be living on the other side of the world. Seeing her father's sad expression made me feel guilty. What am I asking of this family? Is my love for Sabrina a selfish thing?

Cystic Teratoma

Sounds awful, doesn't it? Two weeks ago, an ultrasound revealed that Sabrina had it. Two cysts, as large as my thumb, grew on her fallopian tubes. They cannot be felt from the outside and there are no symptoms. During a reflexology session with her, I came to suspect that Sabrina had a disorder in the reproductive region. (By the way, I am, now a Holistic Health Therapist specializing in Reflexology and Herbalism.) So, she had the doctor perform the ultrasound.

As in most cases, Sabrina's cysts were benign (whew). Still, it is always important to remedy these problems right away. Not wanting to put it off, we scheduled the operation as soon as possible.

72 hours we spent in the hospital. The doctor informed us that it was a simple procedure and that we had nothing to worry about. Having heard that, I put all concerns behind me. At least, I thought I did. Apparently, it's quite easy for the mind to convince you of something you want to beleive. For although I had been cool for days preceding the operation and only paced about the waiting room that day out of boredom, when Sabrina was finally rolled out on her gurney in front of me, and the doctor assured me she was fine, a swelling of emotion rose from within me. I had tears in my eyes.

Dave commented that this may have been a building experience in our relationship. Of that I am certain. Furthermore, as I told Dave, this past weekend in the hospital strengthened my relationship with Sabrina's parents. They had planned on staying overnight with her in shifts, but Sabrina informed them that I would be happy to stay with her all three nights. What's more, I considered it my obligation.

They were noticeably delighted to hear this. When they came to visit, they were also moved by the sight of me doing everything possible to make her more comfortable. Sabrina's mother told her that since the hospital experience, they were much more at ease with her moving to Canada, knowing that I would do my best to take care of her.

Plans

We've been trying to make plans regarding Canada. We're choosing to fly into New Brunswick so I can see some of my old pals and their families. We'll be staying with my buddy, Scotty and his wife, Gloria. I'll finally meet their daughter, Elizabeth. It's about time, considering she is practically my niece. Scotty and I have been as close as brothers since our time together in MacLeod House at the University of New Brunswick.

Following our stay with the salt of the earth that resides in the Maritimes, Sabrina and I will head west to Ontario. Job-hunting will follow celebrations. She may return to the Ad game, while I enquire about teaching positions at the local college. Perhaps, I'll partner with Sifu as a proprietor of our school, should he desire it. As a last resort, Brad will always take me back to the sewage plants (that is to say, "waste-water treatment" plants) of Ontario.

It's comforting to know the plans have been set. After all, who ever implied making plans for your future is a waste of time, must have been an idiot.

This is how I admit I was wrong. Take note of this occasion! As my friends will tell you, it is a rarity.

I'm ready to make Essex County my home again. That is not to say, I won't do any more traveling. Those plans, too, are already being set in motion. But, maybe my restlessness has dissolved enough to allow me satisfaction with short trips rather than epic sojourns.

I have traveled to more than 15 countries, but that leaves an enormous chunk of the world I've yet to see. I intend to experience a few more magical places before I retire.

Brad has finally proposed to Katie. We will be flying to Italy, where they have chosen to hold the ceremony. I, as a non-denominational spiritual minister, will be performing the service. This trip will give me an opportunity to see parts of Italy that I missed on my first visit there. On my list is the church of St. Giovanni e' Paola in Venice. There, I can pay respects to the remains of Marcantonio Bragandino; the defender of Famagusta, who epitomized dedication, determination and devotion - A defeated warrior, but a great warrior, nonetheless.

Returning to that mountain on Ios would be grand. There I made a spiritual connection with a mystic white burrow. First staring at each other with curiosity; he was as surprised to see a visitor with ice blue eyes and golden fleece, as I was to see an ivory burrow. Curiosity gave way to a meeting of the minds and he welcomed me home. Indeed, I felt I belonged, as though I truly was an Argonaut returning to my homeland. My quadrupedal soul-mate won't be there when I go back, but I'm eager to stand on that mighty cliff again.

Sometime later, Sabrina and I will visit friends and family, back here in Taiwan. She'll stay longer as I venture to Mainland China. Beijing and Shanghai hold some interest for me, but mostly I am curious to see the Shaolin temples in Hunan and Shantung. A few experts have informed that true Shaolin Kung Fu does not exist there anymore, contrary to popular belief. Nevertheless, I enjoy a historical pilgrimage. I relish the idea of standing in the very courtyard in which Wong Long developed our system.

Fellow adventurers have told me that other exotic delicacies await me in such lands as Cambodia, India, Nepal and Tibet. As well, Africa captures my interest. I believe no one should leave this earth before witnessing the wonders of Egypt. The pyramids and the Sphinx, of course, would be captivating, but so would a trip to Alexandria, named for the victorious Alexander. Cunning enough to conquer the world and wise enough to win the hearts of those he conquered. From there, Sabrina and I will travel southward. Perhaps, we'll climb Kilimanjaro first and then on to visit Shuan in South Africa and have him grant us the wild pleasure of one of "Captain Corrigan's African Adventure Tours". Perhaps, as a honeymoon… *aren't I the optimistic one!*

As strange as it may sound, even Antarctica is on my list. With great anticipation, I imagine losing my mind in its expanse.

Of course, for now these are just plans. And you know what has been said of plans.

"The best laid schemes of mice and men…"

-Robert Burns

Where I'm Going

There is a wilderness. In it, living, dying and being born, is every creature imaginable, in the trees, in the air, in the waters, and in the earth. Running through this wilderness is a river, strong and soft, cutting through the earth and smoothing the rocks. Standing in that river is a man pushing against it, trying to turn back it s current. The motions of this man are not Kung Fu. Everything else in this wilderness is.

Kung Fu exists in four realms: physical, intellectual, emotional and spiritual. The easiest to cultivate is the physical; followed by the intellectual. With emotional and spiritual, it is always two steps forward and one step back. Often I will awaken to a more enlighten existence only to fall back into a sleepier state of being. I may be playing lively or exercising with fervor, but if you could see my spiritual form it would have the appearance of a swaying drunkard with half-closed eyes.

I am aware that previously I have been more awake; however, as the feeling that accompanies these moments is tied so closely to them, being less enlightened means that I cannot even remember exactly how it felt. This makes the path back difficult. I go through the motions of mediation, cultivation and imagining the expansion of benevolence from within myself. I do this without the feeling, but with sincerity, and eventually it becomes real and I find myself a little more awake once again. Fortunately, it is a little easier each time.

If I return home to Canada, I know that remaining awake will be more challenging. I am distracted by the things I love. Desires are not so much a distraction for me. Would I like a high performance vehicle to drive or a top quality stereo on which to play my music? Sure, I suppose that would be nice. But I like to think of myself as better than a goldfish distracted by shiny things. Family and friends, however, are powerful distractions.

Spiritual monks know that attachments limit spiritual growth. This does not mean that they seek to give up love. Rather they seek to expand their love so greatly that there is no hierarchy of emotional attachment. One loves his friend, his father, his mother, or his teacher, no more or less than he loves a stranger or even a gnat on his skin. Although monks claim not to have goals, they work towards having no attachment to the things with which they are most familiar, not even people. In this, even they fail. Although I suspect they do not fail as greatly as I.

Among my concerns about returning to my home town is my inability to retain much of what I have gained during my years in Asia. How many steps back into "the sleep" will I take?

I don't wish to be a monk! The formations of my friendships were not happenstances. They were conscious decisions to keep certain people in my life – people I consider to be blessings. I refuse to lose them.

Cultivating friendship and cultivating spirit – surely these are not so incongruent!

Returning also means a drastic change in my training. I will be regularly training with others again.

Synchronicity – the word alarms me. For years my training schedule has been my own, with the exception of my courtyard lessons with Sifu Roger. I dance solo through my forms with increased grace and power. How will I falter when asked to perform with a group of twenty or more brothers and sisters?

Sharing – This word also gives me pause. If we emulate our instructors we must instruct. There I have always enjoyed teaching Kung Fu; here I have become accustomed to my selfishness.

At Cambridge, I taught a small group of students the basics just once a week, as part of their extracurricular physical education program. The administration allowed these students only one semester to get a taste of it. – a quick stop in the tiny town of Shareville on my may down Selfish Road.

I know I will enjoy teaching again, but can I give to my students what has been given to me? Can I be an effective conduit between my great teachers and the students? My enthusiasm could be a detriment. In truth, I am eager to share; but I must be careful not to give too much too soon. Sifu Simon has described it as giving a child a plate of food. He gobbles it up and when asked the next day, "What did you have for dinner last night?" he cannot remember.

Confucius spoke with his disciples about teaching methods: "Each truth has four corners. Reveal one corner to your student and allow him to discover the other three on his own." Words for teachers to live by, indeed.

Each student comes into the wilderness hoping to change. This is not to say that all students do not like themselves. All should be there to invent themselves at their best. If they have not come to change they should exit quickly. Many do.

Perhaps, I thought I came to the wilderness just to be more interesting. I suspect I was searching for mountains. My youth was not a difficult one; compared to most, I had it pretty easy. When the universe does not given us mountains to climb, we must find or even build or own. I remind myself that the teacher cannot create the student; he/she must create him or herself. We can only guide each other through the wilderness. Resist the temptation to guide students away from peril. Guide them to the mountain, through the raging rivers and dark caverns. Nourish them; not only on the sweet berries, but on the bitter roots (part of the problem with today's society is that we do not eat enough bitter).

Providing I can remember them, I will offer students the universal truths:

"Look within, you are the Buddha."   - Siddhartha Gautama

"He who knows himself, knows the All" - Hermes Trismegistos

"He who knows himself knows his lord" – Mohammed

"The Kingdom of Heaven is within you and whoever knows himself shall find it. Know your Self."   - Jesus Christ

"Indeed your individual consciousness (Âtman) is Brahma, Vishnu, S'iva, Skanda, Prajapati, the mighty Indra, Kuber, Kâla, Yama, Soma and Varuna." - Agastya

"One who sees himself as everything is fit to be the guardian of this world. One who loves himself as everyone is fit to be the teacher of this world." -Lao Tzu

If I can't remember them, I will offer them anyway.

There are only two things returning me to Windsor: my family and friends, and my Kung Fu school.

And maybe, that's enough.